SUDDEN AWAKENING

August 18, 2005

to my dear John –

Let's wake up!
and live from what
is true, our real home

Happy Birthday
with love
Regina

SUDDEN AWAKENING

into direct realization

eli jaxon-bear

 An H J Kramer Book

published in a joint venture with

 New World Library

An H J Kramer Book

published in a joint venture with

New World Library

Editorial office:
P.O. Box 1082
Tiburon, California 94920

Administrative office:
14 Pamaron Way
Novato, California 94949

Cover design by Mary Ann Casler
Text design by Bill Mifsud
Edited by Nancy Grimley Carleton, with enormous help and support from Despina Gurlides and Tim Nobles

Library of Congress Cataloging-in-Publication Data
Jaxon-Bear, Eli.
Sudden awakening : into direct realization / Eli Jaxon-Bear.
    p.   cm.
"An H.J. Kramer book."
ISBN 1-932073-11-6 (pbk. : alk. paper)
 1. Spiritual life. 2. Religious awakening. I. Title.
BL624.J439 2004
294.5'44—dc22   2004009098

First printing, September 2004
ISBN 1-932073-11-6
Printed in Canada on acid-free, partially recycled paper
Distributed to the trade by Publishers Group West

10   9   8   7   6   5   4   3   2   1

To my beloved teacher, my sat-guru Papaji:
the dispeller of darkness,
the living embodiment of silence and freedom,
the one with the willingness to give everything at first meeting

contents

foreword

When I first met Eli Jaxon-Bear, I knew nothing about *satsang,* a Sanskrit word meaning "association with truth." I found the issue of "awakening" abstract, and I wasn't especially interested. I was leading seminars on personal growth. I was ambitious and idealistic. My work was increasingly successful, and I was basking in the recognition. I had it all together. My life was working just fine.

When I attended one of Eli's open evenings, I came looking for more knowledge and for a new technique. I came looking to incorporate another theory into my intellect. I came looking to add another piece to the puzzle in the work I did with people. Instead, the whole puzzle was taken away from me. In the course of one evening, all of my concepts were exposed as crutches.

I had no idea what "waking up" meant, but in the presence of Eli Jaxon-Bear, I woke up. I awakened from a deep dream of apparent knowledge and security. I lost the arrogance of my mind and won the love of my heart. In the freshest and simplest manner, I came face-to-face with something bigger than any idea, bigger than any name, bigger than any philosophy. I was given the gift of coming to the edge of everything that I could name, and then I was pushed beyond.

To say I was pushed into the unknown isn't quite accurate. It was my own Self, in the form of Eli, that called me into emptiness and fullness. For the first time, in the humbleness, humor, wisdom, and deep compassion of this teacher, I came to recognize my own Self. All Eli did was ask: "What do you really want? If you had to exchange all your many desires for one single desire, what would your desire be?"

My heart knew the answer immediately. It had always carried the answer within itself. It was as if all of my life I had been waiting for just this question. In the simple answer of my heart, all my worlds crumbled, both inner and outer, as those were never in service to my deepest desire for peace and love.

In the simple answer of my heart, I died and was reborn.

By following Eli's invitation, my willingness to let go of the known deepened. I found the willingness to surrender all the countless fights and efforts of my life, so that I could discover what was already here, what is always here, what will always be here.

In *Sudden Awakening,* Eli answers the questions of many seekers after truth, bridging his uniquely deep and fresh insights into modern Western psychology with the profound original wisdom of the "silent tradition." The silent tradition is passed down through a lineage of enlightened teachers. The essence of these teachings is a silent mind.

For thousands of years enlightened beings have pointed to a reality behind the familiar world of appearances. But the experience of awakening, the realization of our true source, seems to have been the privilege of a chosen few.

Eli's clear and simple message, the gift that he offers in this book, addresses everyone: "We live in exceptional times. No matter how difficult it may have been in the past to realize the original Self, now is the time. No matter where you come from, whether you lead a holy life or not, it is possible for you, right now, to wake up. Be willing to let go of everything you think you know, just for one moment. For one moment, be still. In this moment, space and time open. This opening is your chance to find the answer to the question 'Who am I?'"

If you read this book with only the mind, you might take these words for another person's thoughts. But if you have the courage to put aside your judgments and accumulated knowledge for a moment, you will find before you the possibility of waking up to that which is impossible to comprehend through words. Then your very Self can come to you in the form of this book, and speak directly to your heart.

It is the deepest wish of every being to live in freedom and in love. This wish matures in us until we're willing to listen to the call of freedom and to follow it, deeper and deeper.

May all beings be truly happy.

In love and service,
Veit Lindau
Berlin, Germany

preface

In 1971, when I was twenty-four years old, I was hiding out in a cabin in the mountains of Colorado. I was a federal fugitive because I had freed a prisoner and fought with police during May Days, an attempt to stop the Vietnam War by shutting down the American government. At that time, I read the great Taoist classic *Tao Teh Ching* by Lao Tzu. I knew that what I was reading was true, but I had no idea how to get to that perfect tranquility of non-effort. In fact, I couldn't see the point of personal tranquility in a world dominated by genocidal war. I wasn't looking for enlightenment. I was looking for a way to stop the global violence.

Luckily, when pushed against the wall, I found I was not willing to kill to stop the violence. But I was willing to die if that was what it took. Miraculously, one night, terrified and alone in that cabin in the Rocky

Mountains, while praying for help to stop the madness on Earth, I was brought face-to-face with death. Through grace, I passed to the other side: I awoke to the truth of my own nature as empty, immortal consciousness. I knew that if everyone could have this realization, the world would come to peace. I saw this as the great benefit of awakening. I dedicated my life to finding a way to pass the realization on.

Even after the experience of awakening to my true nature, I didn't know how to stop the flow of my egoic mind — the habitual pattern of misidentification that keeps us mired in suffering. I spent the next eighteen years on a quest that led me around the world. In my continuing search for the answer, and in my search for a true teacher who could transmit the answer to me, I had the great good luck to meet and become close to many wonderful teachers of different spiritual traditions. I took my bodhisattva vows with Kalu Rinpoche, and in 1978, he appointed me the president of his first dharma center in Marin County. By then I had sat in profound bliss with Swami Muktananda at his ashram in Oakland, and spent five years with my Chinese Taoist teacher practicing yoga, Tai Chi, and Chinese calligraphy. In the 1980s I spent some time in a Zen temple and after dharma combat in a monastery in Japan, I was presented with a Zen Teaching Fan by my beloved O'Jiisan, of ChoShoJi Zen Temple.

When my mind stopped at the Zen monastery after receiving the transmission of the head priest, profound realizations resulted. In the late 1980s an initiation cer-emony on the coast of Morocco with a Sufi band also stopped my mind, and revealed deep mysteries; psyche-delics and life-threatening experiences had the same effect as well.

But always, no matter how high the experience or deep the silence of the moment, the egoic mind would return with its story and commentary.

These teachers and others gave me many beautiful practices and I still enjoy some of these. I found that some of these practices lead to a disciplined life, which I deeply appreciate. But practice did not lead to deeper realization. All the experiences that arise from practice, although they were beautiful and deep, did not last. For me neither the practice nor the deep experiences perma-nently ended the false identity of the practitioner.

The question that I asked myself back then, at the beginning of my search, is the question I hear over and over again now, more than thirty years later. Most people I meet have already had many spiritual experi-ences. They want to know what to do after the spiritual experience, or the practice session, ends. They want to know how to stay true in the midst of the confusion of daily life, how to not leave that exalted state of peace and love that is untouched by life circumstances.

In this book, I offer you the gift of awakening that was given to me by my teacher, Sri H. W. L. Poonja, a fully awakened *sat-guru* called Papaji. Awakening is real: it is actually the only reality. Awakening is permanent: it doesn't come and go. This gift was passed on to me by my teacher, and this book is an offering of that gift to you. As you read *Sudden Awakening,* you have the opportunity to receive radically new insights into the nature and structure of ego and its role in the creation of suffering.

It is possible that in a flash of insight — a sudden awakening — you will come to understand the prison of mind that we are all born into, and receive the keys to your escape. You will discover that the possibility of true freedom is available to every human being, regardless of life circumstances. My goal for this book is to clearly lay out the choices we face in the search for truth, the traps along the way, the difference between reality and illusion, and the fruits of dying before the body dies as consciousness returns to its source.

Sudden Awakening is for those who are ready for the end of the spiritual quest. I share with you the message of my teacher: It is time to stop the search and realize your nature as immortal, empty, intelligent love. You will receive a transmission in reading this book if you are ready to lay down your suffering and find true, lasting peace.

Welcome!

Eli Jaxon-Bear
San Anselmo, California

a note on language

As cultural experience evolves, we often adopt words from other languages that best express new concepts and experiences. One current example is the word *computer,* which is now commonly used in many tongues besides English.

When it comes to words for the instruments of modern technology, English may have the edge, but it is sadly lacking in spiritual vocabulary. In contrast, the Sanskrit language has always included a vast array of words for describing the spiritual experiences of awakening. For thousands of years the people of India have devoted attention to the spiritual path. To describe in English what in Sanskrit is simply called *samadhi,* we would say, "the blissful experience of plunging within — into the deep experience of your true Self."

In addition, Sanskrit has many names for the different stages and degrees of samadhi, just as the Eskimo have many names for the different types of snow. The culture of India has extensively explored the experiences of the inner world, just as the Eskimo culture has explored the outer world of snow.

Over the past century, the awakening that Indian culture has explored and actively cultivated for thousands of years has surfaced in the West, bringing with it some baggage. Cultural baggage like food, dress, and customs can be left behind, but along with the cultural baggage comes a gift of a rich vocabulary to describe what most of us in the West don't yet have words for. That spiritual vocabulary, like samadhi and satsang, will come to life in the following pages.

PART ONE

THE WAY TO
FREEDOM

welcome home

"**A** life of freedom is possible for you. You can awaken this instant and live as love itself." My teacher Papaji radiated this message to all who met with him in *satsang*. Satsang is beyond the realm of the mind, beyond the reach of any language. Please listen deeply as you read this teaching story of satsang.

satsang: out of slavery

Imagine for a moment that you're living in the time of slavery in the United States. Imagine what it would be like to be born a slave. Imagine that your parents were born slaves, and their parents as well.

Now, imagine for a moment that not only are you a slave, but also that your personal bondage, as well as slavery in general, is going to go on forever. This is just the way the world is. This is what you were born into. You are told what to do. You can be sold or traded at any time. You can be beaten. You can be used in any way.

If you're lucky, you get to work inside the house, or for kind people. If you aren't so lucky, you have to work out in the fields, or for unkind people. This is your life. This is just the way it always has been and always will be.

As a slave, you have probably never been more than fifty miles away from your birthplace. Maybe you've been to another town, but maybe not. There are no televisions, no radios, no newspapers. You most likely can't read or write anyway. You don't know any other life except a slave's life.

Since your parents and grandparents weren't allowed to speak your native tongue, you don't have a cultural past. You may still hear the call of the drum and the secret beat of old tribal songs that refuse to die, but you don't have a memory of being free, and there is nothing around you that points to that possibility. It seems preordained that you and your descendants will live and die as slaves. These are the parameters of your universe.

Within these parameters, you may be allowed to marry or not, have children or not, work in the house or the field, live here or there, but all of these circumstances appear against the background of slavery.

Then one day, you hear a whisper, "There's a freedom train coming."

You may not even know what these words mean. Some of your friends may hear the news of freedom and dismiss it out of hand, as the mad ravings of crazy people. Others may hear the news and say, "Well, I've got a pretty good life here. I live in the master's house. I eat good food. I don't need a freedom train." They are content with the way things are.

Other people, even those who aren't content with a slave's life, may be far too frightened to want to even know about a freedom train because, if they attempt escape, they know dogs will be sent after them. If they are captured, they fear they will be whipped, tortured, and perhaps even killed, to set an example so that no one else runs away. Those who are too frightened to risk these dangers may say, "Don't tell me about a freedom train. I don't want *that;* this is good enough."

Others may worry, "How would I eat if I were free? Where would I live? What would I do if a freedom train took me to a strange new land? Here, I know where I belong. I know where my food comes from. How would I know what to do there? How would I know what to say? How would I know how to act?" They are terrified of leaving the known, and even more terrified of the imagined unknown.

Some may cry, "I'd like to go, but my children are here. They can't go. I have to stay here with my children." Others may mourn, "I'd like to go, but I can't leave because I'm so in love, and my lover can't possibly go." They are terrified of losing the relationships that keep them attached.

But a few hear the whisper, "freedom train," and it's the most important news they have ever heard. They are willing to take the risk to be free, no matter what it takes.

Accepting the call of the freedom train isn't easy. Once you hear the whisper, you're beckoned to put yourself in grave danger just to discover more. You go to secret meetings because you need directions to find this freedom train, and instructions on what to do when you get there. You have to be very careful because you're always being watched. But still, you long to know more. It's a life-or-death situation. You are no longer willing to live in slavery.

Since you've never been fifty miles from home, you don't know the way to freedom. You don't know anything about it. You have to be willing to go alone through the swamp and the woods, leaving everything behind, if that's what it takes. If you carry too much baggage with you, you won't make it; you will sink under the load. So alone and with few possessions, you put yourself on the line and face the unknown. This is the test of fire.

If you can't bear another moment of slavery, regardless of the cost, regardless of the risk, you heed the instructions, follow the trail, and find your way to the freedom train.

This is the end of identification as a slave and the beginning of a life of freedom.

the map and the destination

First, satsang is the whisper. This whisper lets you know that it is possible to escape from slavery. Some people can't bear anything more than simply to hear about this possibility. Just to hear this good news — that freedom is possible — is enough. It may take years, or lifetimes, before they are ready for the next step, but at least now they know it is possible.

This is the first function of satsang: the announcement of the truth of freedom. Sometimes you have to hear it over and over again. When you've heard that freedom is possible enough times, and this possibility sinks in fully, eventually you fall deeply in love, and attaining freedom becomes the very purpose of your being.

Second, satsang is the map, the path, and the way to find the freedom train. Satsang provides the direction to follow, and warns of the traps and pitfalls along the way. Satsang points out the confirming signs, as well as the dangers of getting lost. Satsang shows you your current location, describes the ultimate destination, and points out the quickest route for getting there.

Third, satsang is the freedom train itself. It is the end of your burden. Once you're on the train, you don't have to carry your luggage on your head; you can put it on the rack and sit down. You can stop everything and let the train carry you. You can put down the burden of slavery, and surrender to the grace that carries you home.

Finally, satsang is the destination: it is home. It is freedom. It is where you arrive. How long does it take to arrive? It depends on how far you have wandered away from yourself.

Eventually, when you arrive, you laugh at the deep realization that there never was a leaving; it was all in your mind. You sold yourself into slavery in your mind. Since you never really went anywhere, how long can it possibly take to return?

the sweetness of coming home

Satsang is your own heart speaking to you in silence. It is nourishing, sweet, and true. This sweet silence comes and carries you home.

Satsang is the mirror in which you see yourself — in which you see at last who you are, and who you are not. When you know who you are, you realize the great benefit of stopping your false identification as a slave. True freedom is being your Self. Satsang reveals the truth of your Self and the way back to a natural life, free from the slave identity.

When you look back from the shore of freedom, you see that you were not who you thought you were. Who you thought you were didn't transform into something else. It never was. It was all just a nightmare of slavery passed on for generations, a nightmare of the ego's separation, alienation, and loss of love, which has ended as suddenly as awakening from a dream. In this awakening you can accept and love life as it is.

Looking back at a dream from awakened consciousness, you see the perfection of even the dream. You see the non-separation in the appearance. You realize yourself as the living truth of immortal love. Then life begins.

CHAPTER TWO

what do you really want?

In any life, essential questions emerge that demand answers. The answers determine the course of your life for good or for ill.

I remember being faced with such a question when I was an eighteen-year-old freshman at the University of Pittsburgh in March 1965. I had the good fortune to be present when a phone call came in from a neighboring college letting us know that a bus was heading down to Montgomery, Alabama, to take students to join the Student Nonviolent Coordinating Committee in marching for civil rights in the face of great violence. The question everyone asked was "Are you on the bus?"

My answer was instant and deeper than any thought. Andrew Goodman, a boy from my neighborhood in New York, had been found murdered and buried in a swamp with two other SNCC workers the summer before. A white northern minister on just such a bus, Reverend James Reeb, had been beaten to death a day before on the streets of Selma, Alabama. Police were turning marchers back with dogs and water hoses. People were being violently attacked and thrown into jail. This was a terrifying situation full of unknowns, and I was an upper-middle-class Jewish intellectual who had led a relatively sheltered life. All of my family and friends would call me mad if I got on that bus. I would be putting my life in danger; I would miss school and possibly flunk out; and I would end up on an FBI list, ruining my future career options. Yet I knew without a doubt that I was "on the bus." The gift and clarity of that choice gave me the confidence to not look back.

Gradually, my choice in favor of freedom, even in the external political way that I defined it at the time, pushed me to my limits. "Really?" freedom would ask. "What about this situation? Are you willing to compromise here? Will you hold steady there?" Inch by inch, year by year, I came to see what my life was about and where I was heading. I was forced over the cliff of the known world. Getting on the bus represented a much deeper commitment than simply enduring a few weeks of dangerous adventure. Finally, I had to give my life fully to getting on the bus for freedom without a thought of getting off. The bus at that point embodied a commitment to walking the talk. Freedom asked: "Are you willing to risk death to stop the suffering in this world?" When the miraculous answer "Yes" appeared, the necessity of facing death opened the way for me to cross the ocean of illusion and receive the truth of my own Self.

Getting on the bus was a choice that led me forward on the path toward freedom. Other choices I have made led in a different direction. When I followed my desires and called it freedom, I found this led to deeply painful consequences. Like me, you have faced life-altering choices: whether to stay or go, whether to have children or not, whether to follow what is in your heart or cling to the safety of the known. You can look back now and see the results of the choices you have made. You can see the precious moments you stayed true to yourself in the deepest way as well as the times you betrayed yourself and followed the norm. Each of those choices leaves a mark — sometimes in the form of a wound, or a reinforcement of fear and doubt, and other times as a revelation of the deepest essence of soul. All of your choices, whether fortunate or unfortunate, are useful. Each shows you something important about yourself, and all are allies in helping you face the truth.

the essential question

Now I pose this essential question to you: what do you really want?

Surprisingly, most people have never asked themselves this question with any depth. Indeed, most people live their entire lives without really questioning what it is that they truly want. Most just make do with whatever shows up. Most are content to settle for some version, hopefully a little bit better, of what their parents had or wanted. Others may rebel and strive for something totally different from what their parents had, but end up with the same results. Many people who choose to become parents say that what they most want is not to treat their children the way their parents treated them. I can appreciate that. I chose not to have children in this life partly because I didn't want to pass on the suffering that was given to me. But all these choices exist in the realm of relative slavery. These are not true choices, but conditioned responses.

When we are acting out of conditioning, all of our choices are rooted in a ground of ignorance. Unless you know who you are, all of your choices remain the choices of a slave. Of course, slaves sometimes protest that they are in fact free and can do whatever they please. Except be still. Slaves do not have the power of silence. Silence is the key that unlocks all of the chains of slavery. All slaves are bound to the noise of arising phenomena. In using the term *slaves,* I am including the roles of both master and slave, since all roles in this world are roles of relative slavery. The apparent master is as enslaved as the apparent slave. Both are addicted to sensory experience and to the voices of their egoic minds talking in their heads.

My teacher, Papaji, says that there is a river of thought waves, and all beings are being washed downstream by this river. Some rationalize that they are going with the flow, others zigzag and imagine that they are in control, while still others gather objects and people around them so they can float down the river together. The rarest of the rare are those who give rise to the desire for freedom. Freedom is the willingness to take a stand exactly where you are, in the middle of the mind stream.

This desire for freedom cannot be contained. It cannot be moderated. It cannot be tailored to the expectations of others. When those who are washing by in the stream cry out that you are lost, that you are falling behind as they rush ahead, great temptations surface that urge you to turn away from your true Self and swim back into the mainstream. But the desire for freedom is not a casual affair. It is the culmination of the spiritual path. It is the end of the search. It is the end of life as you knew it. So you do not waver.

My teacher would look into the eyes of seekers who said that they thought that they wanted freedom and demand, "If your hair were on fire and you were rushing to the river, and you passed some friends who called out to you to sit and join them for a cup of coffee, would you stop? Would you even take time to answer? No, you would keep heading straight for the river! That is the desire for freedom. There is no time to sit and think."

Examine yourself and see what is on your own personal list of what you want. For most people on the path, the list goes something like this: "Sure, I want to be free, but I also want to be successful. I want to have money. I want my parents to love me. I want to have great sex." None of these desires is bad in and of itself. It is simply not the way to find true freedom and happiness. Ask yourself honestly: has changing your circumstances, changing your partner, or having more ever led you to lasting peace and true fulfillment?

If you still believe that changing something in your life will make you happy, you aren't yet ready to find true happiness and freedom. But perhaps someday, when you have exhausted all of your attempts to fulfill fantasies, you will finally be disillusioned enough with the world to look somewhere else. A faster, more direct way to freedom and happiness is to go through your list of preferences and desires right now and see that none of them are ultimately fulfilling, because they are all desires of the slave. Then you're ripe. Then you're left with one single desire, the desire for freedom.

This desire turns into a blazing fire, because it is the only desire. It takes hold of you. This burning desire for freedom is like a funeral pyre. It burns all of the elements that made up your false identity as a slave.

Then everything is revealed. You fall into a realization of yourself that is beyond your wildest dreams. The depth and the duration of your experience in this vast realm of realization depends on the intensity of your desire. The more you surrender, the deeper it takes you, and the longer it lasts. This is the samadhi mentioned at the beginning of this book.

This, too, disappears, as all experiences come and go, but you are left with a certainty that is revealed through experience yet is beyond experience.

At some point, everything that you turned away from comes back to test you. If you don't touch the temptations, they too burn in freedom's fire, and your realization goes even deeper.

the desire for freedom

Again, I ask the question "What do you really want?" I repeat this question because you can accomplish nothing of real consequence until you answer this question on the deepest level. Once you answer this question, a radical reappraisal of your life may point you in a completely new direction.

Most people's lives are dedicated to getting what they *think* they want. The problem is that most people don't know what they *really* want. Most people live in the conditioned wants of family, and in the manufactured wants of society, with their subconscious fantasies projected onto the world. In this way, they spend their lives invested in false wants and desires.

Most people only know how to define what they want by what they already have and what they don't have, by what they want to fix or get rid of, by what they want to keep or increase. All of this, including all relationships, belongs to the realm of objects, but ownership of these objects is only the projection of the egoic mind. This egoic mind, which tells a story to itself about who it is, feels separate, alone, and cut off. Caught in the habit of misidentification and suffering, it is desperate to defend its space.

People caught in the egoic trap constantly avoid what they really want. But so long as there is an experience of separation, there is a correspondingly deep and true longing for union. So long as there is fear and a sense of isolation, there is a deep and true longing to return home.

My counsel is to tell the truth about where you have turned away from the longing for union, so that you can find time for the deep and true call of your heart. Until you allow all the self-betrayals to be unveiled in the light, you subconsciously sabotage what you really want. By self-betrayal, I mean every place where you have sold out or settled for something less than the deepest truth of your heart.

Be willing to stay true to your deepest longing for truth, in the face of all the subconscious pulls that arise from the ocean of mind as thought waves trying to wash you back into the desires of the subconscious.

In the end, the desire for freedom transcends all other desires. It is the only true desire of a human life.

Being aware of having this desire in the past was very rare. But humanity is now entering a new stage. Either we will evolve quickly or we will destroy the Earth. The choice is ours. Now is the time for ordinary people to wake up. There is no need to be a great saint. Simply because you are alive and intelligent enough to read this, you are ready for the next evolutionary leap: from the isolated selfishness that is destroying the world to the bliss of union, which holds the healing of the Earth. Perhaps the only hope for the planet lies in our willingness to end our personal suffering.

Until the desire for truth, freedom, and love arises in a life, everything is pointless. Life is all about "me" and "my" story of "reality." Once the desire for freedom arises, it becomes the central axis, the ground of being that life revolves around. This is the beginning of the end. It signals the end of the search and the birth of realization.

Awakening is the end of wanting and the beginning of discovering.

spiritual maturity

When you're caught in the enslavement of egoic identification, you're convinced that there is both a "me" and a world, and that you have to do something to manifest the good and keep away the bad. This "me" seems to be the ground of your being. This "me" has good times, and this "me" has bad times. You would like to hold on to the good times and get rid of the bad times.

As you mature, you realize that the good times always come to an end. Short-lived pleasures inevitably carry the aftertaste of long-term suffering. Think about it. In examining joys of the past, can you say that your joy ever lasted? In anything you have ever enjoyed, has your joy ever really been enough for you to say you are fulfilled and need nothing more? Circumstances change, and when they do, you lose the emotions and states that were caused by those circumstances. Loved ones die, jobs change, money comes and goes, and with the flow of circumstances your mind is lifted up and crashed down over and over again.

Every ego wants to keep the highs and get rid of the lows, but wisdom lies in seeing that you never find true fulfillment, joy, and happiness this way. Causeless joy is unconditional; it is not determined by the ebb and flow of circumstances. Recognizing this is one of the hall-marks of spiritual maturity.

Once you realize the nature of suffering and the possibility of freedom, you become willing to turn away from every idea of who you think you are to find the truth. In this truth, you discover the joy that does not fade or change with circumstances.

For most people, "ignorance is bliss." Most are content to have as much pleasure and as little pain as possible. What they are really expressing is the desire to extinguish self-consciousness and return to the life of an animal. This is the desire to pull the covers over your head and try to sleep, ignoring the monster that is in the room with you.

But for the spiritually mature, those who are ripe with the readiness to realize the real and the true, this avoidance no longer works. To the degree that you're mature and ready to end your suffering, to that degree you become aware of your deep and genuine longing for home.

We live in exceptional times. No matter how difficult it may have been in the past to realize the original Self, now is the time. No matter where you come from, whether you lead a holy life or not, it is possible for you, right now, to wake up. Be willing to let go of everything you think you know, just for one moment. For one moment, be still. In this moment, space and time open. This opening is your chance to find the answer to the question "Who am I?"

I am here to tell you that if you picked up this book, if you found your way to these words, you are ready to know the answer to the essential question of your heart. You entered this collective dream with one purpose and one purpose only: to wake up and realize the truth of the situation — that you are formless, timeless, immortal love, and that you're already home.

PART TWO

THE NATURE OF
REALITY

CHAPTER THREE

metaphors for the
human condition

In part 1, I told the story of the slave hearing about the freedom train for the first time. Here are some additional metaphors that convey the flavor of the human condition and set the stage for our exploration of the true nature of reality.

chicken-dancing

Some time ago, I read an article in the *New Yorker* magazine by Calvin Trillin that evoked a childhood memory. In the 1950s, when I was growing up in New York City, my family would sometimes go to Chinatown. There was an arcade there with three different boxes of performing chickens. For a nickel, a curtain would open, "Turkey in the Straw" would play, and a chicken would come out and dance to the music. If you put a nickel in the next box, a chicken would emerge who would play the piano. A nickel in the third box brought out a chicken who would play tic-tac-toe with you. At the end of each performance, a slot would open and the chicken would get some corn.

To some degree, everyone in the world is like those chickens performing for corn. Perhaps the chickens dancing to the music feel superior because they are expressing themselves in their bodies, while the piano players are proud of practicing their art and feel special because of their emotional sensitivity, and the tic-tac-toe players feel superior because they are using their minds, not their backs, to get food.

Do you wonder whether these chickens ever feel an existential longing for the flock? Or are they too busy dancing for corn to notice that things are not as they are meant to be? Are they perhaps too smug, feeling that they have the world at their feet, offering corn galore, to wonder about the true nature of reality?

The three bodies of human identification represented by the chickens — physical dancing, emotional piano playing, and mental tic-tac-toe — are expressions of the styles of addiction to chasing corn; they veil true essence. A conditioned response, whether it is dancing for corn or putting on a tie and going to work, is first programmed, then internalized, personalized, and made into something special. When something is personalized, it becomes part of an internal story explaining and rationalizing why you are doing what you do. All human beings performing the various rites of chicken-dancing think that their performance is special, and they are hurt when others don't see it that way. By identifying your *act* as yourself, you feel proud or ashamed, lauded or misunderstood, and never notice that all this is taking place as you scratch for corn.

We live on a slave planet. Everyone here has been conditioned since birth to personalize the scratching for corn. This is the prison of mind that keeps everyone in line, busy at the food chute, and missing out on life.

Some farmers have learned that barnyard music makes animals more docile on their way to the slaughterhouse. Humans have personalized their own channels of barnyard music. This is the talk radio that runs, seemingly nonstop, in your head and also in conversation with others, commenting on "me" and "my" circumstances, deciding which life choice to make, all the while lining up for the corn that leads to slaughter. Everyone is whistling in the dark and dancing as fast as he can, on the way to the slaughterhouse.

It is time to stop chicken-dancing, bring the barnyard music in your head to a full stop, and discover that which is prior to all movement and all noise. Then, when the impulse to scratch for corn arises, you have a choice about whether to follow it again.

the metaphor of movies

The great Indian mystic and sage Ramana Maharshi often used the metaphor of movies to explain the nature of reality. You watch a film, and on a barely subconscious level you know that what you're seeing is only colored lights. But that level of reality has to be ignored in order to enjoy the experience.

You laugh and cry and get involved in the movie as if it were real. All the while, it's really just a light shining from the projector. To see this light requires turning your back on the movie. But if you're busy identifying with the story of the movie, you don't want to tear your eyes away from the screen. To perceive the truth of the situation, you have to be willing, for one moment, to turn away from the movie totally and completely, and look toward the light.

our own private movie

Your own private movie is called *Me and My Life*. The projector is what we call the mind. The mind is a prism; it is crystallized consciousness of a certain density. Light shines through it and gets refracted and projected into the world as "*me* and *my* objects" or "*me* and *my* relationships." For now, let's call the invisible light that shines through the mind to project your world the light of your soul.

You play your part in the world. You live in it and you die in it, again and again. Countless times, all of humanity lives and dies in this projection we call reality. Humans are terrified to turn attention away from the movie, let alone leave the theater. Until one day, through grace, you hear of a world outside the theater.

The world outside the movie shatters the wildest imagination of the mind that is watching the movie. It is beyond the mind's capacity to grasp.

Perhaps another way to experience the metaphor of movies is to imagine that movies are being advertised for the first time, before anyone has actually experienced one. You don't know what to expect, and neither do your neighbors. Let's suppose that the first show is being promoted like this: "Come sit in a dark room with a hundred strangers and have a vicarious experience that may involve sex and violence." This advertisement might attract some people to the theater, but not most of the average movie audience.

For movies to work, you have to ignore the fact that you're sitting in a dark room with strangers, and focus instead on the story unfolding in front of you. In a similar way, ignorance and denial work in the ego structure as you make believe and ignore reality.

When I speak of turning around and facing the light, I am not speaking of just one more idea in your movie, or of changing reels or movie theaters. I am speaking of the essential unreality of all movies. When you abandon all identification with the movie of "me and mine," you see what is left. When identification with everything disappears for a moment, the real *you,* the one Self, continues living as individuated consciousness — but with more intelligence and greater presence, finally at peace.

Later in this book, we will delve deeper into the dynamics of the egoic mind, which offers up the movie that leads us to ignore reality. Keep the movie metaphor in mind as we also unveil the soul that is always here, always calling on us to turn around and face the light.

CHAPTER FOUR

out of nothing

Human life is such a fleeting, rare, and precious moment. Mysteriously, as human beings we have the capacity both to reflect on our own mortality and to realize immortality. To make our human lives worthwhile, to reach the fulfillment of our highest potential, we're called upon to discover and recognize reality. Reality is *that* which does not come or go, *that* which does not appear or disappear, *that* which was never born and never dies.

In our world, which is a tiny planet orbiting a relatively small star in a remote corner of a minor galaxy, life arose rather recently. When we look at it in the larger scheme of the universe, human life on Earth has really just begun. And how much longer we survive on this planet may depend on whether we wake up *now*.

the reverberation of "i"

The main contribution of the Judeo-Christian tradition to the cross-cultural phenomenon of the creation myth is this: In the beginning was the Word. And the Word is with God. And the Word is God.

Instead of *Word,* let's use *thought:* In the beginning arose a thought.

The thought is "I." This thought, "I," is with God and this "I" is God.

"I" is the thought that is exploding as the universe. This thought of "I" arises from emptiness and is a reflection of emptiness. As a reflection it seems to be different from emptiness. But since the emptiness before the birth of the universe includes everything, how could anything be separate?

Both the universe and the mind aren't separate from, or fundamentally different from, what they reflect. Just as a tiny piece of a hologram contains within it the complete picture, so the reflection contains the whole and is held by the whole. All comes from the one thought, "I." No tiny piece, no giant galaxy, is separate from this first thought, "I," not even you.

Everyone says "I." "I am that I am!" is the first declaration of God to the prophet Moses. This comes down to us in the first of the Ten Commandments: "I am the Lord thy God" is a bad translation of "I Am That I Am."

"I" echoes as the sound of the universe. It vibrates in every subatomic particle and in every galaxy. In Sanskrit this sound is called OM.

the one cosmic being

Time and space are created with the first thought, "I." This thought solidifies into dimensions and realms of energy and matter. The universe gives birth to itself as the form of the one cosmic being. This being expresses itself through all form. Each individual is a unique prism in the one "I" of God. Each of us is a flavor of the personality of the Godhead.

The one cosmic being has an infinite number of cells — souls, galaxies, star systems, planets, humans, insects, dust, atoms, subatomic particles — everything from the most macro to the most micro levels of the universe. Thus, the cosmos is similar to the human form, which is made of countless cells, with a myriad of different functions and differing life spans. Millions of your red blood cells are dying and being born as you read these words. These cells, for whom *you* are the cosmic being, depend on your grace and good judgment to keep their universe alive.

The cosmic being we call our universe has nurseries where new stars are born and new galaxies come into being. It has old, burned-out suns and black holes, which suck in time and space. These cycles of creation and destruction reflect themselves in all dimensions. In our cultural trance, these cycles are reflected in gardens and day-care centers, and in burned-out neighborhoods that suck the life out of the air. They are also reflected in each of us personally, as we have both nurturing tendencies, where we give birth to new creations, as well as

emotional black holes which seem to drain the very life
out of us.

Both as the formless and in the form of the universe,
the cosmic being is waking up out of the starry slumber
of unconscious dreaming. The cosmic being has given
rise to itself as reflective consciousness, with the capacity
to realize itself in form. This plays out at the level of you,
the reader. You have the potential to awaken from the
dream, and to realize the truth of yourself as the formless intelligence we call the cosmic being.

a brief scientific mythology of the universe

For a moment, let's examine what comes and goes, what
is born and dies, to see how and where we have misidentified that which is impermanent as reality.

Before the universe comes into being, there is no
time, no dimension, and no space. Often this condition
is called emptiness, since the mind cannot conceive of
that which is prior to everything.

Out of total emptiness, the appearance of form
emerges. This first form arises as a single, tiny dot,
which then explodes as the Big Bang. This dot is continuing to explode today. Everything that is present
now was present in that dot. The universe is the
expanding of the explosion of that dot. There is nothing in the universe that has been added to or is separate
from that tiny dot. This dot is the thought, "I!"

The first explosion of the Big Bang can still be

heard and seen today with the right instruments. The edges of this explosion mark the boundary of our known universe. It is the edge we can't yet go past. It is both our womb and our trance.

In truth, the perceived universe is simply the arising of an appearance in emptiness. It isn't permanent. As with all thought, it was born, and it will die. The only question is how and when.

Emptiness is always empty even within the appearance of a universe, because the universe, arising from emptiness, must necessarily be made of emptiness. There is no permanent substance here. Whenever you look closely enough, substance becomes slippery and then disappears.

Matter that appears solid is only a temporary appearance; it can also appear as a wave of moving energy. The material universe is constantly in flux, appearing and disappearing. Yet we persist in treating the world as solid and real, because we believe ourselves to be solid and real.

The universe, if taken as solid matter, can never yield the secret of that which is before creation, just as living in and minutely exploring the inside of a bubble never reveals the secrets of life outside the bubble, or the bubble's creator. However, the universe is much more intelligent than inert matter. It functions to awaken the dreamer to the truth of reality prior to the arising of the form of the universe.

The universe is an intelligent design that gives rise to organisms, in our case human beings, who are capable of intelligently investigating the paradoxical experience of form transcending all form.

the ingredients of life

In our universe of birth and death, the first stars exploded long ago. The fiery core of the early stars cooked the simple gases of the cosmos to produce larger, more complex atoms such as carbon. As carbon-based life, we humans are living as the charcoal briquettes of the early suns.

Cooked in solar ovens, building blocks of life rain down on countless worlds. On Earth, life arises from a process in which the simple chemicals in the primordial sea eventually assemble into genes. After many millions of years, associated genes band together and work to create a barrier to protect themselves, and the first one-celled organisms are born. A one-celled organism is the first space suit for survival. Some of these one-celled organisms evolved while most remain the same. Earth is still primarily populated by one-celled organisms that we name bacteria, plankton, and so on.

Humans are an advanced confederation of cooperating cells, such as blood, brain, and liver cells, gathered together in a protective sack called skin. We can look at humans as a collection of cell colonies gathered inside a gated community, with a feeding tube open at one end to receive nutrients, and an elimination tube open on the other end to release wastes. Is this what you refer to when you say "I"?

awakening from the trance

We were all born into a trance that we have learned to call "reality." Most people take for granted that reality is what they can see, feel, touch, taste, and smell. We know that as human animals we see only a very small spectrum of light, flanked by an enormous electromagnetic spectrum of lower and higher frequencies, including infrared, ultraviolet, microwave, X-rays, and gamma rays, which we can't see.

What if we could see farther out on the spectrum? We would see auras and the streaming of energy. We would see that there are no hard edges, and that everything is energetically flowing into everything else. Would we call that reality, the way we call what we see now reality?

What about what we hear? What if we humans could expand our limited range of hearing so that we could hear what bats and dolphins and the great whales hear? Would our definition of reality change? The whole universe is sound vibrating at different pitches, rhythms, and frequencies. The overwhelming bliss of directly experiencing the sound of the universe is sometimes revealed in moments of extreme absorption into the true Self. What if we could hear the movement of the heavenly spheres?

If the universe is an appearance, and what we see

and hear are but a tiny fraction of that appearance, what is reality?

As human animals we live our lives in a very small spectrum of experience, calling it "my life." As formless consciousness, we have the capacity to discover the truth behind the appearance. We can see through the trance to find the source.

light in the darkness

In Hindu mythology there is a cosmic being, Vishnu, who exists prior to all universes, and remains when all universes have returned to emptiness.

Out of the navel of Vishnu arises Brahma. Out of Brahma arises the universe. According to this ancient creation story, there have been untold countless universes, each one arising out of and returning to Brahma — as countless Brahmas arise from and return to the navel of Vishnu.

Each time Brahma shuts his eyes, we have the cosmic night and the darkness of untold eons. When Brahma opens his eyes, the universe is flooded with light, and golden ages of wisdom and kindness flourish.

According to this wisdom tale, we now find ourselves in the *Kali Yuga,* an age of darkness. The good news of this plight is that it is much easier to see the light in a darkened world. In the midst of the horror of darkness, this light is perpetually shining, always and forevermore calling us home.

CHAPTER FIVE

maya's veils:
the trance of mind

In Sanskrit, the trance of mind is called the play of *Maya*. Maya spreads her veils of illusion, obscuring the light and casting shadows. In pure light, there is no illusion. In absolute darkness, no forms appear. Only in the shadow land of reflected light do the forms of the world appear in their ever-changing dance and play.

The light of consciousness is ever present. Its apparent veiling of itself reflects its own power to create an illusion of a universe — all so that it can meet itself, see itself, and love itself.

understanding the secret of maya

A student was sitting under a tree with his teacher on a hot day in India when he asked to understand the secret of Maya. After expressing some reluctance, to test the student's readiness, the teacher replied that he would answer the request if the student would fetch him a cup of drinking water from the well in a nearby village.

The student went off to the village and waited his turn by the well. The most beautiful woman he had ever seen was standing just ahead of him in the line. He had never seen anyone like her before. He knew in his heart he had met his soul mate. She was the perfect match he had always secretly longed for. Emboldened by his surging heart, he spoke to her. Remarkably, she felt the same way about him. They both expressed the thought that it was destiny that they meet this way. The young man asked her to marry him, and she agreed, but only if her father would grant this unlikely request at a time when all marriages were arranged between families.

So the young woman brought the young man home to meet her father and ask his permission. The young man was very afraid and not sure what to say. But as soon as he entered the girl's home, he felt at peace. It felt so warm and homey that his nervousness slipped away. He was greeted by the family as a long-lost son. The father agreed to the marriage on the condition that the couple stay in the village. In return, he would give them a wonderful farm to live on. The young man agreed.

The couple had a splendid marriage ceremony and soon moved into their new home. The father had supplied everything for his daughter's happiness. They had farm animals, good land, and a perfect home. They loved each other, and they loved the land. Soon they had children, first a son and then a daughter. This was the life the young man had always dreamed of, but that until now had seemed impossible to attain. He and his wife were happy and shared a blessed life together.

This bliss continued, until one day a huge roar exploded from the mountains as a storm unleashed a powerful flood. The family heard the noise and began to run. The young man put his daughter on his shoulders and took his wife by one hand and his son by the other as they tried to make their way to higher ground. But the water overtook them. Their house was crushed and washed away. They found themselves waist deep in water as they watched their animals being swept away before them. Suddenly, the son lost his grip on his father's hand and slipped into the rushing water. In grasping to save him, the daughter fell off her father's back. As the young man reached for his children, he lost hold of his wife's hand, and she, too, washed away.

The young man could not believe the tragedy that had befallen him. He wept with pain and anguish at his loss as the raging waters swirled around him. He was filled with hatred at the forces that had destroyed everything he loved. As he cried, his tears dropped into the swirling, muddy water. Drop by drop as his tears fell, the water became calmer and clearer. He then heard a voice in his ear saying, "Where is my water?" In a flash he realized that he was crying into a cup of water by the well. He turned and prostrated himself before his teacher, for he now deeply understood the nature of Maya.

the mystery of maya

Perhaps we all have had the experience of looking out to the end of the ocean where it seems to meet the sky. Even though our reason and our knowledge may tell us otherwise, it still seems as if the ocean and the sky meet in a straight line at the very bounds of the Earth. Similarly, when we look up, we see a blue sky. Even after we've flown high in the air and seen that there is no color there at all, the sky continues to appear to be blue.

These optical illusions, similar to a mirage of water that we sometimes see in the desert, represent only a superficial display of the power of mind. The trance of Maya makes the sky appear blue and the Earth seem flat. On a more fundamental level, the trance of Maya makes matter appear solid and real. The trance of Maya hides the true reality of formless intelligence, as an open secret in the midst of contrary appearance. The trance of Maya represents one of the greatest powers of mind.

The only greater power of mind is conscious silence.

The great mystery of the trance of Maya is its ability to make the insubstantial appear substantial, and to give rise to the appearance of a "you" and a "me." From the mind's great power to create the appearance of something from nothing, the first thought, "I," arises, as we saw in the last chapter. This first thought, "I," is reflected in the countless prisms of all life-forms like a multidimensional funhouse mirror.

Once there is an "I," a world appears. Within this world, countless "you's" and "me's" are born and die, in massive, continuous waves. Each one born calls itself "I." The mind plays the same trick whether it is creating the birth of the universe or the birth of a child.

For each person on planet Earth, there are about 900 billion stars containing countless planets and undoubtedly myriads of life-forms. How significant is a human life in the cosmic scale of things? Yet each tiny blip we call a human life vibrates around a central core of "I." If you investigate the root of the thought "I," and then leave all thought behind at the gateway of the unknown, you come to recognize the true "I" and awaken to the final realization.

the appearance of duality

The trance of Maya is the appearance of duality. First, duality is the experience of separateness from a defined other — whether this other is "nature," "creator," "beloved," or simply "them." But even more than separation from this other, duality is the experience of separation from your true Self.

This duality serves a purpose. Although duality gives rise to ego, as we will explore more fully in part 3, it also gives rise to the path to freedom. While duality may lie at the root of suffering, it also offers the path back to unity.

hosts for dna

We can view the relatively recent development of the neocortex, where our higher cognitive powers seem to reside, as an advanced survival strategy over the reptilian brain. An early-model reptile brain is an essential part of the human body, and it still plays a vital role in the regulation of our survival functions. The more recent evolutionary additions of the limbic system and the neocortex represent upgrades, leaving the reptilian brain running underneath, undisturbed. Even as you read this, your reptilian brain is regulating your body temperature and the inflow and outflow of your breath. The human animal can survive severe damage to the newer parts of the brain, but without the reptilian brain stem, it dies. Do you think of yourself as an advanced reptile when you say "me"?

From one perspective, what we call a human being is really a survival machine constructed through countless incarnations of DNA. Intelligent design meets natural selection through an elaborate interplay with the environment. Design imperatives of the genes require countless strategies for everything from survival of the organism to courtship rituals and nest building, so that the DNA gets passed on.

The DNA codes in each of our cells have been

around since the chemical soup of early Earth first gave rise to complex molecules. Yes, our DNA has been living continuously, passed along from entity to entity since the days of the primordial sea! In a very basic sense, our bodies are mere hosts for our DNA, and our DNA is relatively immortal.

Since the human body is a survival machine for DNA, from the point of view of evolution the persistence of DNA is more important than the life span of the human body. Once the duties of the sperm-and-egg game are fulfilled, passing on the DNA to its new host, the original form can eventually wither and die with little loss to the gene pool. In fact, the form's eventual death makes space for the offspring to continue and multiply.

And this entire production is Maya's display.

separation and individuation

I read a report recently that a group of scientists believe they have discovered a genetic mutation that enabled articulate speech in humans. This mutation may have occurred as recently as fifty thousand years ago. They theorize that the first humans with this mutation were so successful in surviving that it spread very quickly through the gene pool.

Being able to speak articulately gave such a survival advantage that it would have led to the dominance of one group of early humans over another, depending on which gene pool was carrying the mutation. If this theory is correct, then we are the descendants of this small band of genetic mutants.

Closer examination reveals that the capacity for speech also gives rise to individuation. When Adam, in the Hebrew Bible's retelling of the Mesopotamian myth, names the animals, he is separating himself from what he names. There is now an inside and an outside, resulting in enormous power as well as enormous alienation. A direct experience of separateness from the world now reigns. This separateness brings with it a greater capacity for survival. Being one step removed from the world, through the power of naming it, humans develop more sophisticated strategies for dealing with food, danger, and sex. Soon every human gene line contains the coding for this power of separation.

the evolution of "me"

The arising of a "me" represents a great leap forward in the survivability of form. Survival means two things: persistence and replication. Whatever supports persistence and replication is rewarded. The abilities to get more food, to avoid being eaten, and to replicate quickly and without error are all rewarded. The egoic sense of the independent doer is the latest upgrade to the genetic survival machine. The egoic sense of self has power to override circuits and make strategic choices that enhance the survivability of the form. We are born into a ruthless play of survival. From the one-celled being on there is a drive to survive in order to pass on to the next generation all that came before. The egoic "me" was so successful that every human had to have one.

Our stories are simply attempts to explain, justify, and make meaning of our lives, with a fanciful overlay that overlooks millions of years of genetic impulse. Our present condition is obviously due to forces that go much farther back than our parents.

Out of separation and individuation arises the idea of someone in control. The so-called separation-individuation process in babies and toddlers describes the stage where the world comes into view, as they move out of amorphous blending with the primary caregiver and start to differentiate.

Separation and individuation mark the birth of the "doer," who can override the reflexive survival circuitry of the human body. Now there is the appearance of someone in charge who makes choices from a larger perspective. Since this ability is highly effective from the evolutionary perspective, it, too, spreads through the gene pool like a virus. The software program called "me" becomes necessary for survival.

If Maya is the producer and your genes are the directors, determining, for example, what you find attractive in a mate, what you look and smell like, and what looks and smells turn you on — determining everything from your subconscious nest-building survival strategies to how well you take orders — what role do you imagine *you* have in Maya's play? How much control do you really think you have? Who wrote the lines you're thinking, the roles you're performing?

What if you're not really in control at all? What if you're only a minor character, tightly scripted and directed by subconscious forces, here for a mission that has nothing to do with you in particular? My teacher said that there is only one true choice in a life; all the rest is conditioning. That one true choice is to turn your back on everything to see that which is prior to it all.

separation and individuation in cultural myths

Separation and individuation have also found expression in many of the fundamental myths of Western culture.

adam and eve

The biblical Adam and Eve represent the human face of individuation. They are the mythic first relatives who spoke the first words. As father and mother, they spawn countless generations with the once-rare mutation of speech and its attendant powers.

Naming the animals is the first power. With the inflated sense of self that this power brings, Adam and Eve are said to defy God by eating from the Tree of the Knowledge of Good and Evil.

This act results in the awareness of duality: good and evil, Adam and Eve, God and "me." The egoic inflation of Adam and Eve increases out of the arrogance of breaking God's rule and surviving. This is what the Judeo-Christian tradition calls "original sin." Most egos have replayed this original sin down through the ages, as rebellion against the voice of the angry judge in the head — a voice thought to be God's.

In acquiring the knowledge of good and evil that leads to differentiation, the soul now experiences itself as torn from God. Humans feel separate and ashamed. Trapped in the duality of mind, torn between good and evil, the soul searches for a way back to union.

What remains untouched in the center of the garden is the Tree of Immortality.

the myth of lucifer

The myth of Lucifer is the myth of the egoic mind, caught in judgment and blame. Tired of endlessly praising God, Lucifer rebels. Since he would rather rule in hell than serve in heaven, Lucifer, whose name means "the bringer of the light" and who served as God's favorite angel, is flung into the dark recesses of a far corner of the universe to make his way slowly back to God.

According to biblical legend, along the way home Lucifer makes deals. The egoic, controlling mind trades in money, sex, and power for survival, pleasure, and prestige. The cost is the immortal soul. We turn from the light of the soul and focus on the objects that are shining in the light of the eye. However, it is only the reflected light of the soul that gives these objects their desirability.

During this journey, Lucifer discovers that life is hell because he can no longer hear God's — his beloved's — voice. God's voice is overshadowed by his own voice barking commands, voicing opinions, and talking to himself.

As Maya's trance deepens, each ego plays the role of Lucifer — the doer, and the ruler of its own kingdom. Each ego turns away from the bliss of divine union in order to be in control. This is the genetic imperative for the unit to survive. A separated, alienated ego is a tool or weapon for propagating DNA. But it comes at a high price.

In the separation from our true source, we are deprived of the nourishment of true knowledge, the fruits of the Tree of Immortality that still stands at the center of the garden. We thirst for the divine nectar, but are never able to quench our thirst. This, too, is hell.

Each soul is called upon to return from the hell of isolation, from playing the doer and the judge, to find its way home. The agony of hell contains within it both the pain of separation and the bliss of return.

the arising of the superego

When Adam breaks the only rule he has received, he is representing all of us as our first father. The rule appears as the voice of God arising in the egoic mind. Not God as empty, open, intelligent love, but rather a vengeful God who metes out judgments, rules, and punishments. Freud called this the superego. The superego judge is the guardian at the gate of deviance.

From the perspective of genetic programming, the superego is a master fact-checker. It holds the idealized blueprint of perfection and checks for flaws. This judge is constantly comparing choices to an internalized standard derived from outside expectations. The standard is not internally generated; it comes from a higher source, whether called God, Mother, Father, or Church. This standard is a survival circuit patrolling the neural pathways, weeding out deviance, which is a form of mutation. Mutation usually does not pay off for the early adapters, since most mutations introduce random patterns that radically decrease the chances of survival. The superego stays with the tried-and-true.

With the arising of the superego, the primal duality of Maya — God and soul — is internalized. Now an imaginary doer — the ego — makes decisions, which are constantly judged by an angry voice in the head — the superego — which calls itself God, Father, or just "what is right."

In order to increase the odds of both survival and replication, the human animal masks the internal warfare between the doer and the judge with a superficial layer of personality designed to cover what is really going on. Then we humans spend our time focused on the personality, which is just deflecting signage, without addressing what is really running the show just beneath the surface.

shame and deflation

Adam's breaking of the rule causes him to experience a terrible fear of retribution, which becomes part of the fabric of the egoic mind. Guilt and shame arise next, to take their place in the egoic underworld as the interiorized experience of deflation.

Most people spend their lives avoiding the deep feelings of terror, shame, and despair by living on the surface, engaged in trivial pursuits. But the lucky ones can't avoid the pain, as it slaps them harder and harder to get their attention. God will gladly take all of your precious holdings — your relationships, your power, and your health — whatever is required for you to begin your journey home.

In Adam and Eve's case, God evicts them from the garden of Eden. They are suddenly cast out of the garden in shame. Now, instead of the animal flow of unity and instinct, they experience themselves as someone separate, someone judging, someone who feels bad. According to the Bible, they look for something to blame, with Adam blaming Eve, and Eve blaming the serpent. The horror of their human predicament punctures their egoic pride and the inflation of feeling special.

Homeless and without prospects, Adam and Eve set off to face the unknown.

Shame is part of the birthing of self-consciousness. It alienates us from God and nature. Shame can only arise in the trance of separation. When we meet shame head-on, rather than avoiding or shunning it, shame can lead to the opening of the deepest grace. When you know this secret, you bear the pain of wounding in the willingness to die for truth. Shame can pull you inside, toward home and the end of trance. Shame can lead you to your true Self, which in fact has always been right there waiting for you.

Falling into the negative emotional states of deflation — and surrendering into the willingness to die to know the truth — leads to emptiness and realization.

Unfortunately, the egoic mind, in a desperate bid for survival, tries to deflect this falling inside. It gathers attention and, instead of going within, thrusts outward, leading to rage against God and against circumstance for the whole mess of incarnation as an animal. Outward thrusting of rage and defiance leads to a new inflation, inevitably followed by deflation, just as, in the biblical myth, Cain murders Abel out of jealousy and rage. We are the descendants of the killer.

the origin of religion

At some point in human evolution, supernatural religion arises. It is clearly an advantage to the gene pool if the defenders of the DNA are superior fighters, willing to risk their lives for the defense of the tribe. If warriors believe that they have a god or gods who are protecting them and will take them to paradise when they die, they fight more fearlessly and more ferociously than if they were terrified of death. Religious warriors have an edge in battle, because their confidence in otherworldly forces makes them much stronger than other warriors.

A belief in a supernatural religion becomes an advantage to the gene pool and eventually spreads throughout the human species. In this way, humans may unknowingly breed themselves with a genetic impulse toward a belief in supernatural beings.

religion, writing, and calendars

Along with religion, writing begins to develop, and with it the sense of time changes. Because there is a record of the past, humans no longer live in the present. They create calendars, noting the earth's rotations around the sun as years. They further divide time into months, which mark the rotations of the moon, then into weeks, days, and hours. All of these divisions modify our experience of time, giving a sense of reality to what is passing illusion.

What year is this? Everyone reading this book knows the answer. This is a question evaluators ask of patients before they release them from a psychiatric facility, to prove that they are sane.

But have you ever examined the answer more deeply? Where does it come from? Why are the seventh and eighth months of our calendar year named after the Roman emperors Julius and Augustus? Why are Thursday and Friday named after the Norse gods Thor and Freya? Why is the Hebrew holy Sabbath named Saturn's day? If the Chinese, Mayan, or Hindu empires ruled the world, what day and year would this be? Since Jesus lived and died under the Hebrew calendar, which started 3,500 years before he was born, what year would this be for him? We all live in a global trance of time and space. This trance is a spell, and a spell is simply a word of power.

As we know, the current calendar was developed as a form of religious and political control, first by the Roman Empire and then by the Catholic Church. Pagan gods such as Thor, Freya, and Saturn were co-opted to bring the "savages" into the empire. What are we actually counting when we say this is the year 2004? The number of times planet Earth has revolved around the sun since a Jewish boy was perhaps born in Bethlehem, give or take a few years?

What was it like when a few hundred years ago Pope Julian changed the calendar to the one we know today? One day people were living in a certain year, and the next day they were living in a completely different year. New Year's, which people once celebrated in the spring, now takes place in the dead of winter. How arbitrary can it get? If instead we measured time by how long it takes our solar system to make one turn in the Milky Way galaxy, which is thirty million years per rotation, what year would this be?

By keeping the dates small, by not counting the millions of years it takes to make one rotation around the Milky Way, we give greater importance to individual humans and their short life spans. This is an important part of the ego inflation that the process of individuation entails.

the evolution of religions

With most of the world in a deep trance, a few people wake up to the realization of the truth. The impulse to know God actually breaks through the tribal trance, allowing a few people to discover reality beyond the known or imagined world. They experience the realization that in truth there is only one mind, one consciousness, revealing itself in all form.

But over time this realization becomes conceptualized. A concept is a thought that can be held on to, and replaces the actual experience. Those who have never experienced oneness can now say, "Of course there is only one God." Belief in one God becomes the "modern" religion, trumping the gods of tribal magic. Monotheistic religion then spreads around the globe, knocking over the small gods and goddesses in its path. The equilibrium established by each tribal gene pool having magical gods that control the weather and every-day events is now overthrown by the one God who is above all others.

In the Judaic-Christian-Islamic tradition in particular, the adoption of a monotheism that asserts that all other gods are false is a breakthrough strategy for cultural and genetic conquest. Judaic-derived monotheistic religion proposes a belief in one God as an entity somewhere else, called heaven, who is watching and listening to each and every one of his faithful. This belief stems from a misunderstanding of the truth of the one cosmic being that is alive as all form, and as the empty formlessness from which all arises.

the cargo cult mentality

Primitive superstition regarding how the world works is still with us today. We can look at ourselves entranced by our fantasy of a remote God and a material universe as similar to the cargo cult mentality of primitive people trying to comprehend what is beyond any of their conceptual models. The cargo cult phenomenon arose during World War II, when downed airmen in New Guinea enlisted the natives in building a runway and lighting it with torches. Soon a giant metal bird dropped from the sky, bringing the people gifts and taking away the strangers. For generations after, people continued to build runways in the jungle and light them with torches, waiting for the metal bird to return.

from the cult of religion to the cult of personality

Most people today are still living in a cargo cult mentality. They believe in one God, whom they worship and supplicate to do their bidding while trying to follow his rules. This one God lives somewhere else and looks down on everyone, sometimes interfering in their lives and sometimes answering their prayers by doing what they want. This is the cult of religion.

When this primitive form of egoic projection is taken seriously in the world today, we see the horror of the consequences in religious warfare. Religious people all around the world — Buddhists, Hindus, Muslims, Christians, Jews — are killing one another over a certainty that there is one God and he is theirs. Recognition of this horror signals the beginning of the end of the worldwide cult of supernatural religion. While it may have served in days gone by, it is no longer in the interest of the gene pool to have this belief. It's time for this cult of religion to die out, or it will destroy us.

As human culture recognizes the horror of the trance, there is a deepening despair and alienation. At the beginning of the twentieth century, some proclaimed the death of God as the destructive power and killing capacity of the human animal increased. Life is seen as expendable on a scale never before conceived. Morality is senseless. The rules no longer matter. Kings are overthrown, but still society is corrupt, even under the rule of law as opposed to the rule of God and king. Nothing makes any sense. Life seems pointless.

Out of this despair emerges the cult of personality, in which money, the body, and the individual ego are worshipped. Alienation reaches its peak. This is the next crucial stage of individuation and heralds the evolution of consciousness, even though it is still mired in illusion.

Full alienation isn't possible until you are disillusioned with religion and society. Alienation is the separation of individuals from their subconscious identity with the herd. It is the emergence of individuality out of the muck of the primordial sea.

Alienation is a necessary part of the individuation process. It clears the field for the reality of God to burst through the ego's borders, and for the imagined narrow boundaries of mind to explode into the unknown. Now there can be a conscious return to the source. Consciousness emerges from the background, from the underground, from the bottom of the ocean, to look at itself in wonder.

Here on Earth, DNA has evolved from producing a one-celled space suit to a complex sack of chemicals that can now reflect back on itself. As we intelligently examine and discard our attachment to the name and form of our particular sack of flesh, we discover that what is left is who we truly are. What is left when all identification with form is dropped is who we are prior to all appearance. Intelligent conscious inquiry into the nature of reality and into the nature of trance is the way that individuated consciousness returns to its source.

It is important to know that there is a possibility of something beyond what is believed to be reality. Even though the truth is beyond description, it has to be spoken of so that the possibility is made known, like the first whisper of the freedom train I wrote about in chapter 1. Even if you were to discover that there is nothing beyond normal human experience, you still would have nothing to lose in the inquiry. But if what I am telling you is true, then you have everything to gain.

PART THREE

SOUL AND
EGO

CHAPTER SIX

the call of the soul

O ut of the fire of creation, sparks fly in all directions. The spark is not in truth separate or different from the fire, just as the soul is not different from the empty field that it arises from. Yet, since it is a subtle form, the soul experiences a sense of separation.

the nature of the soul

The soul is the condensation and crystallization of immortal consciousness from a dimension before relative time and space. It is made of emptiness, awareness, and love. These aren't distinct and separate qualities, but rather flavors of one taste.

In modern usage and language, the soul has many names. The word *soul* itself means "only," or "no other." It also means "the sun," which is the source of life. Immortal self, higher self, essential self, and true self are also names for soul.

Sanskrit, too, has many names for soul: A *jiva* is a soul enmeshed in ego. When this soul awakens, it is called a *jiva-mukta,* or liberated soul.

After establishment in its pure state, the awakened soul is called *atman,* the immortal Self. Atman goes in search of *Brahman,* the source of the universe.

After awakening, the great Indian mystic Ramana Maharshi went off to find his beloved mountain, Arunachala. Jesus went in search of his Divine Father. First the ego returns to the soul, and then the soul returns to the source. These are the natural stages of awakening.

The awakening of the soul is the purpose of life. The soul awakens from its identification with form, and returns to union with God.

The soul incarnates by identifying with its denser forms. The soul is a condensation out of emptiness. It produces within itself denser and denser forms. Egoic identification is the mirror of soul. All calls itself "I."

"I" arises as a thought from soul, as soul is the "I" thought of God. Since all this happens with the mirrors of reflective consciousness, the levels reflect one another endlessly.

the story of the soul

The soul reincarnates again and again as ego, searching for home while being tossed and turned by the momentum of its past karmic waves of desire and fear. The suffering ego that searches lifetime after lifetime for happiness is looking outside itself for fulfillment. Eventually the egoically identified soul feels the wounding of the world, hears the calling of the heart, and returns home. It finds that the only way home is discovered by turning within.

At any moment in an egoic life, the call of that which is deeper can arise. In truth, the call is always there. All are called, but few listen to the call, and even fewer respond. Of those who respond, fewer still are willing to give everything to it.

Giving everything to this call requires the return from the self-important somebody back to nobody at all. This is the divine mystery of the revelation of the personality of the Godhead. Individuated, unique personality returns to its homogenous source. Then the individuated personality is a prism that conscious love shines through. What was once the problem of ego is now unveiled as the prism of soul.

Realizing yourself as pristine emptiness is the greatest gift of grace in a human life. Returning to the realization of oneness is the fulfillment of this stage of human potential.

the role of wounding

Depending on the density of egoic defense, humans usually don't hear the call to return until they experience a great wounding or complete alienation.

Most people have to fail enough, or succeed enough, to know that fulfillment will never be found in the realm of appearances. We have to be smashed and crashed by the waves of the karmic sea to want to seek refuge and lasting peace. We have to see through enough of the world's lies to hunger for the truth. We have to see the meaninglessness to seek the meaning.

This is spiritual ripeness. My teacher, Papaji, would say that it takes a mountain of merit, accumulated over countless lifetimes, to be lucky enough to hear the truth and to have the capacity to respond. In the past, most people who reached this stage of ripeness did not experience the grace of hearing the truth. Instead, they got snared by religion and cults, which use the concepts of truth mixed with superstition, beliefs, commandments, and sins to herd the flock.

Having no religion, no rules, and no path offers a shortcut to essence. However, this shortcut is not a casual affair. It is rare, for there is much pain for humans to experience as they encounter the gatekeepers of fear and doubt. Very few are mature enough to realize that through their willingness to bear what is here now, and through facing the fear of death of the body, they may find true fulfillment beyond measure.

Perhaps the increasing environmental signs that life is dying on planet Earth will provide the secret trigger that opens the floodgates of realization to the whole human population. Who can say? In any case, it is certain that ordinary human beings, without being born avatars or saints, now face the possibility of waking up, heeding the call of the soul, and realizing the deepest, most profound truth of the human condition: that they are unlimited, immortal consciousness aware of itself.

CHAPTER SEVEN

stages of ego development

What is an ego? There is an old Hindu teaching story about a cow-herding boy who one day loses the rope for tying up one of his cows. He goes to the village wise man, who tells him that after tying up the other cows, he should make believe he is tying up the rope-less cow as well. This works, and all of the cows stay in their place all night long. The next morning, however, all of the cows head to pasture except the one without a rope. The boy returns to the wise man, who advises him to make believe he is untying the imaginary rope from the night before. Sure enough, this works. The story tells us that the ego is the imaginary rope that binds the cow. I would add that the identification as a cow is what allows the belief in the rope.

first specialness

When a baby is born, it can't see the world around itself very clearly. The spatial coordinates for clear sight take some time to develop. People who are born blind and receive corneal implants later in life require a great deal of time and experimentation to learn to see the world the way most of the rest of us do. At first, the formerly blind don't see edges. One way or the other, we have all *learned* the very boundaries we take for granted and assume to be real.

Babies start with no sense of an inside or outside. They chew on their own feet as if they were foreign objects. If they are lucky, they first see and imprint on the mother's eyes and breast. The mother becomes the first object of fixation. For babies, the mother is God the creator. She is the protector and provider of milk. She is the all-knowing presence who is there when needed. She can anticipate needs and fulfill them. The way she functions meets all of the egoic needs for a God.

Learning to see the world in a given way is a process of fixation. It is a genetic function, part of the survival of any animal, including humans. As the baby's worldview falls into place, the inside remains a vast empty blackness, which the child does not consider consciously. This emptiness lies quiescent in the background, the place the baby goes to sleep. The baby's attention is focused outside, on the Mother/God. Being loved by Mother/God gives the baby a sense of ego inflation, or first specialness. This is the initial state of ignorance.

Since many babies never have the experience of a loving Mother/God on the outside, the stage of first specialness can also result in ego deflation. Lack of love creates an unquenched thirst, and a sense that the child is undeserving and uniquely unlovable, since "God" is not providing.

Either way, whether its ego is inflated or deflated, the baby develops a sense of specialness. Someone unique, either loved or unloved, is now present as the center of the universe. This unique someone now tries to get its needs fulfilled from the outside. The ego has emerged. The ego builds a sense of "me" with defined boundaries, separate from the world. Now, instead of vast blackness and emptiness within, there is emotional turmoil.

first wounding

At some point, every baby experiences its first wounding. This wounding might take the form of a harsh word, a mean look, a physical blow, neglect, or maybe some other action or inaction on the part of the Mother/God. The baby does not know that its mother isn't really God, but a sleepwalking young woman enmeshed in her own neurotic preoccupations.

This wounding by Mother/God pierces the ego's inflation, or reinforces its deflation, and in either case leads to deflation and alienation. Now the child experiences separation and hurt where there was once a sense of limitless, oceanic love.

This pattern of inflation, wounding, deflation, and alienation continues through the stages of maturation. The young child either submits and learns to do what is required to avoid the wounding, or it rebels. Submission, fueled by fear and self-loathing, produces rage. Rebellion, run by arrogance, lust, and pride, produces fear. Either way, the ego is now fixated around the wounding, and either in reaction or submission to the outside.

The essence, which was once at the surface, is now buried under the wounding. The wounding is further buried under emotional reaction. Instead of feeling the pain of the wound, the child experiences anger or fear. On the surface, a compliant child may appear smiling and well-behaved, but just underneath can lie a reservoir of rage. The rage may cover hurt or a fear of rejection, which in turn covers the hopelessness of the situation. Under this hopelessness lies deep despair covering a black hole of dead emptiness. Finally, under this black hole is essence in its latent potential.

As the child grows, defenses start forming to fend off future wounding. Personality develops. The ego devises strategies for not provoking further wounding by establishing outer boundaries to hide behind and mechanisms to provide what the child wants from the outside. The ego also develops strategies for not feeling old wounds by establishing inner boundaries so that the child doesn't feel the depths of pain and despair.

Slowly the ego builds an outer wall and an inner wall, and the child finds itself more and more isolated, living inside a shell. The child moves toward the outer wall when inflation energetically pushes up and out. Pride, arrogance, being right, and feeling special are all flavors of inflation. The child moves toward the inner wall when a sense of deflation and disassociation pulls back and down. Feeling separate, depressed, listless, numb, and spaced out are all styles of deflation. With deflation, the ego retreats from the outer world, but also avoids the deep inner world, floating somewhere in between. Whether these walls of the ego are built around compliance or rebellion depends on the genetic momentum of the child.

crystallization of the fixation

At some point in the child's development, an egoic fixation crystallizes. The specific crystallization is genetically predetermined for each child. Just as a poodle puppy grows up to be a poodle even if it is raised by a German shepherd mother in a German shepherd litter, so a child's fixation remains the same regardless of environment. The fixation crystallizes when the child is around three to five years of age, when the proper circumstances — often traumatic — present themselves.

The crystallization happens in one of three bodies — the physical body, the mental body, or the emotional body. The spiritual teacher Ramana Maharshi called this crystallization "the knot of ego." The immortal Self has no ego sense and does not suffer. The inert physical body has no ego sense and does not suffer. Mysteriously, between these two the egoic sense of self arises and crystallizes. This false self suffers, and the cutting of this egoic knot — the end of the belief in the false "I" — is freedom.

the evolution of consciousness

All of our egoic life consists of the noise of the movement of mind, imagining a past and a future. The egoic mind is constantly talking to itself, measuring, comparing, and sifting through accumulated past events trying to make sense of an unknown future. When the mind is still, the egoic identity, like the universe, disappears.

The material universe and the egoic identity both reflect the trance of mind. The mind's great power gives rise to this phenomenal illusion so that consciousness can evolve to reflect on itself.

There is no "you" separate from "everything else." You, as an ego, are a part of the totality, whether you experience it or not. This can be compared to a fingernail that may have no conscious realization that it is a small part of something greater; the fingernail's ignorance does not change the fact that it is part of a larger whole.

You can realize your oneness directly, if you're willing to investigate your unexamined attachment to your egoic identity as someone separate.

At first you may want your personal sense of yourself to be so big that it contains everything, but it doesn't work that way. Then *you* would be at the center of the universe, and everything would be *your* object. This is inside out — similar to the ego inflation of young children who expect the world to always be the way that they want it to be.

The "I" that wants to be at one with everything does not exist. It is a reflection of reality, but not reality itself, just as a mirror reflects your face but is not your face.

If you realize this and stay true to the realization by not indulging your selfishness, then there is no place for the egoic "I" to live. If you give up knowing and doing, you discover that there really is no separate "I." Then you see oneness everywhere.

There is no outside, and there is no inside. These are only defense mechanisms of the egoic "I." Find out who you are. Find out what is real. Otherwise, all of this is merely a concept that you play with so that you can justify having a more spiritual "I" that feels connected and at one.

Jesus used the metaphor of the rich man who couldn't fit through the eye of a needle. This parable means you have to leave everything behind — that is, all of your attachments — and turn to the unknown. You have to abandon the idea of "me" and "mine." When that idea disappears, pure clarity shines.

CHAPTER EIGHT

the structure of the ego

Now that we have a clearer sense of the soul and of the ego, let's look more closely at how egoic identification veils the essential qualities of the soul, and explore the ways ego and personality keep us locked in a trance of "me."

veiling of the three essential qualities of the soul

When you realize the truth, you encounter the three essential qualities of the soul: awareness, silent consciousness, and the bliss of love. An unveiled soul in Sanskrit is called *sat chit ananda,* or "being that is conscious bliss."

As the ego identifies itself with the physical, mental, and emotional bodies mentioned in the last chapter, this process of identification veils an aspect of essence.

awareness

Awareness, or *sat,* is the first quality of the soul. It is a fluorescence of being. Being is reality. In truth, there is only one being, beyond religion, concept, or belief. You can't teach or learn being. Even the *sat-guru,* the final teacher, does not teach being but is the radiant manifestation of the truth of being.

Being is everywhere, at all times, in all directions, completely homogenous. Being is your very nature, but if it gets veiled, then you mistake the physical body for being. Then you call yourself a "human being." This is the first obscuration, the first falling asleep. The ego imitates being by thinking and trying to figure out what to do, or by learning the rules, or by just acting out the animal drives and calling it "going with the flow."

silent consciousness

Silent consciousness, or *chit,* is the second quality of the soul. It is veiled by the thinking mind, which is filled with fears and doubts. The thinking mind tries to imitate the wisdom of silent consciousness by processing information and planning the future to keep things safe. The ego calls this mechanical neurotic voice "intelligence," even as it veils true intelligence.

the bliss of love

The bliss of love, or *ananda,* is the third quality of the soul. It is veiled by the emotional body, which is rooted in self-hatred. Knowing itself to be flawed, the emotional ego hates itself, feels in need of love, and searches for it on the outside. It attempts to get love by manipulating the personality, making it seductive, helpful, successful, or whatever else is required to get love.

ego and personality

For true essence to shine, the veils have to be removed. The way to accomplish this is through intelligent self-inquiry, which leads to a deep understanding of how you have misidentified yourself as an ego. Every ego begins with the belief "I am a body." This misperception is a form of false identification, and represents a fall from grace. On a deep level, consciousness is aware of the pain and despair of being trapped in a body, and this causes rage, fear, and self-hatred. These are the root emotions of all egos.

Every ego imagines itself to be an island. What is "me" is on the inside. What is "not me" is on the outside. The ego can't exist without separation and boundaries.

The island's shore is the personality. The personality is the sum of the conditioned responses, as the inner drives of the physical body (rage), the mental body (fear), and the emotional body (desire) meet the karmic circumstances of a particular lifetime. The energies of these three bodies mix with the drives of survival, sex, and relationship to mold the personality, resulting in an interface between the inner and the outer.

The personality is the most superficial layer of self. It is the outer edge of ego. Personality can be seen throughout the animal kingdom. Anyone who has spent time with cats, dogs, horses, and even chickens can see the different personality of each individual. Studies in Costa Rica have shown that ants exhibit personalities as well, ranging from lazy ants who avoid work to others in the same colony who behave more aggressively.

Most people spend their time trying to improve or fix their personalities. In itself, this is relatively harmless, but it is usually a sign of narcissistic preoccupation. Such people manage to avoid deeper issues or cover them over with spiritual platitudes.

From a cultural perspective, some personalities function better than others. But from a larger perspective, no personality is perfect, and each is perfect as it is. The deeper truth is that perfecting the personality never leads to ultimate fulfillment or realization.

Papaji used to say that working on the personality is like holding the curly tail of a dog to make it straight —

an interesting exercise, but once you relax your hold, the curl returns!

the secret controller

Behind each personality is the secret controller; this is the next layer of egoic identity. The controller is "the knot of ego," where pure, formless self is bound to an inert body. This ego puts on different masks of personality to suit the circumstances. The secret controller can be friendly, seductive, distrusting, or angry, depending on the role, the characters, and the environment. This is the ego masquerading as God.

This ego rules in a hell of its own mind and circumstance, instead of serving in heaven. It has a story filled with rationalizations and excuses to avoid facing the deeper structures that are actually driving all of its decisions. It is terrified of surrendering control, even though surrender of control is the gateway that each person is called upon to pass through to realize the truth. The secret controller behind the personality calls itself "me," and says, "This is my body, that is my name, this is my past."

In an attempt to transform separation into oneness, the ego searches for someone to share its island with. But this search is doomed, since each ego is only the appearance of a different, separate island. There can be no true sense of oneness for the obsessive-compulsive, fearful, needy "me."

the three drives

The needy "me" of the ego is run by three drives imprinted in the DNA: a survival drive, a reproductive drive, and a social drive (which surfaces as the drive for power). Again, as we discussed in part 2, all of this is organized around ensuring that the DNA and its evolving genes survive and multiply. The three drives, which operate just below the surface for most people, rule the life of every organism. Most of your decisions are made subconsciously to satisfy one of them.

For example, if your subconscious motivation is survival, then all your choices will be based on security — determining which man or woman is a safe partner, which job is the most secure, which friends you feel safe with. Your conscious mind develops an elaborate story to rationalize all the decisions you make from the subconscious motivation of avoiding the terror of experiencing danger.

If the social drive is preeminent in your life, you find yourself completely enmeshed in your family or social group relationships and don't even notice that this is so, just as the fish swimming in the ocean doesn't notice the water.

If your sexual drive is primary, you probably believe that your aliveness derives from your sexual energy, and you arrange your life to serve that belief.

Through the power of mind and the trance of Maya, when you say "me" you're not considering the space in each atom, or the survival goals of the DNA. You don't think of the drives for survival, sex, and social relationships. Rather, you form an amorphous idea of a "me" based on identification with your body, your thoughts, and your emotions, and a story of the past, the present, and the future. This story is contained in thoughts, pictures, memories, feelings, and sensations, woven together with a central narrator. This is the trance of "me."

the trance of "me"

The egoic trance of "me" shows itself in three different veilings of soul. As I mentioned in the last chapter, each ego is crystallized in one of the three bodies of manifestation:

- THE PHYSICAL BODY: *fleshy and filled with rage and laziness*
- THE MENTAL BODY: *electric and based in fear*
- THE EMOTIONAL BODY: *fluid and based in neediness*

All of us share in common the experience of having a physical body, a mental body, an emotional body, and an encapsulating egoic identity that includes all three. Perhaps you never looked at it this way before. Up until now perhaps you just said "me" without consideration of what "me" really meant. In this case, every time you spoke you were subconsciously referring to these three bodies along with your personal story that weaves it all into a whole fabric of "your" life.

Being ignorant of the three different bodies and the egoic identity that claims the bodies as "mine" does not mean the three bodies don't exist. As we uncover ignorance and examine the layers of consciousness, we're discovering what is already here — that which is not manufactured by thoughts or imagination, but by the subconscious structure prior to conscious thought. *Subconscious* simply means that it is floating somewhere beneath the surface of conscious awareness.

By identifying with the veilings of the physical, mental, and emotional bodies, you overlook the soul's essence. Identification with these bodies veils the "being that is conscious bliss" of sat chit ananda, and obscures the light of essence. This light is still shining, but the veils create distortions. You see the shadow, not the light. But, even when you experience shadow, the light of the soul is always there, just as the sun is always shining even when clouds temporarily block the appearance of light.

the voices in your head

All voices in your head belong to parts of the ego. The doer who asks "What should I do?" and "What do I want?" is the ego. The judge who makes rules and blames self and others is the superego. The basic duality between the doer and judge is the egoic internalization of the soul and God. The ego plays the rebellious soul who is determined to be in control, while the superego plays God.

The ego then either follows the rules of the superego and feels rage, or breaks the rules and feels terror. You spend your life in the realm of these voices and the decisions that arise out of them.

Something deeper is calling you. It is not a voice. It is the call of your heart. You don't know where it is going to lead you or what the outcome will be, but you know for certain that it is beyond choice.

If you feel a desire to come home, you're experiencing your Self calling you home, calling you to cast off all that veils essence. Since the mind also wants to come home, it learns to quiet itself and to trust. Since the emotions also want to come home, they, too, learn to trust.

Let me ask you: Do you have the courage to follow this call, to trust that which is deeper than the mind? Do you have the courage to unveil the splendor of essence?

treatment and healing

Once you call forth your courage and begin to understand the traps of the ego, how do you find your way home?

psychology and the ego

Sigmund Freud, the father of modern psychology, was the first major thinker in the West to identify the existence of the subconscious and the structure of ego, but he had a limited view of treatment, and no idea at all about the way home. He believed that the most that psychology could accomplish was to remove neurotic patterns so that a person could have a healthy ego to cope with the misery of life. He brilliantly described the basic hopelessness of the situation, but he did not see a way out.

One of Freud's students, the Swiss psychiatrist Carl Jung, developed a psychology that went deeper. Jung recognized that there is one true Self, and that the ego's job is to return to the Self by learning about and somehow integrating the symbolic structure of the subconscious sea. However, he worked with material that surfaced in dreams rather than developing a method to explore the subconscious directly.

The Sufis' approach to healing the ego, hundreds of years earlier, was to explore the recovery of essence through practices such as whirling, which stimulates a direct experience of transcendence.

In our time, in the West, we can heal egoic wounding by means of insight into the deep structure of mind. We can now see that despair resides at the core of every ego, because at its root the ego is empty, and this emptiness is experienced as loss. Despair covers the essence that has retreated into the depths. The ego senses that the situation is hopeless: life is meaningless, filled with unbearable pain and fear. Death is coming, and there is no escape. If you are willing to experience this directly you will discover what is deeper. You will find that death and despair are covering a secret exit out of suffering. Let's examine this in more detail because most of us were taught to avoid death and despair at all costs. Instead we hide in the superficial.

If the mind is a lake, and the water is clean, clear, and still, then you can easily see whatever lies in the depths. However, once you throw a thought into the lake, this thought makes mind waves that ripple across the surface, obscuring the depths and what lies hidden there. These mind waves are waves of fear and desire. As long as fear and desire are making waves we cannot see the underlying despair. As long as we do not experience despair we miss the secret opening beneath despair that drops into emptiness.

layers of emotion

In our culture and time, when people come close to the truth of impending death, they become depressed. In becoming depressed, they lose the willingness to continue participating in the rat race. Our Western mainstream solution is to medicate the symptoms, so that people can avoid the despair, move back up to the surface, and become productive again. A return to shallowness is a return to surface emotions, to the stories of victimhood, or to a spiritual trance of positive affirmations.

Egoic emotions are layered one beneath the other. Most people spend their lives in the emotions closest to the surface. The emotions they are experiencing are usually not true emotions at all, but ones manufactured by their personal story. Thus, people live in nervousness and anxiety instead of fear, in pressure and frustration instead of rage, and so on.

Usually, when you experience a true emotion, you also experience — almost immediately — a thought giving meaning to the emotion. In this way you avoid the direct experience of the feeling through mental conceptualization. Projection, rationalization, inner dialogue, numbness, denial, and disassociation are all strategies for avoiding the direct experience of negative emotions. You touch only briefly upon the emotion before the ego bounces back into a mental story of personal meaning.

However, if you're willing to bear the emotion without adding a thought, you discover in the direct experience that the emotion is covering a more deeply nested feeling. You have been avoiding this deeper feeling even more than the one above it.

Under anger, there is usually hurt and sadness; under sadness, fear; and under fear, despair. Each particular egoic fixation is wired differently, with a slightly different layering of emotions depending on its unique construction of avoidance. In all cases, however, the way to return to essence is by allowing yourself to fall down through the entire parfait of emotions.

While it is possible to drop directly from any emotion into essence, taking this kind of shortcut generally means that the layers of emotions you avoided on the way down through the subconscious reappear to serve as tests that try to pull you back from the essential state. For example, if you drop from sadness directly to joy, the fear, rage, and despair you haven't experienced, along with corresponding thoughts and circumstances, rise up in an attempt to pull you back into believing the trance of the personal story. If you don't move back into incarnation in the story of those emotions, but meet them directly without thought, they burn away to reveal the shining immovable essence that you are.

staying present

The way we keep our mind waves of fear and desire subconscious, or hidden from conscious view, is by avoiding the present moment. In the present moment, everything arises. Avoidance consists of endlessly thinking about the past, planning the future, or having conversations with ourselves about what we should or shouldn't do, or what others should or shouldn't have done. All this talk, both internal and external, deflects from the essential, and allows us to avoid meeting the subconscious wave that is present in the moment.

A great spiritual trap occurs when people say they are "just in the now," when they are still subconsciously identified as a body, and still unaware of all the waves rippling across the surface and through the hidden depths below. This is simply ignorance covered by spiritual jargon.

To truly "be here now" means to invite to the surface everything that you have been avoiding. Death is the final guest to enter the present moment. When you meet death fully and realize that which does not die, you have returned to your source as immortal Self.

Only then can you be fully present, incarnate in form, to meet whatever arises.

inviting despair

Rather than staying with the superficial layers of emotions, you can embrace the possibility of inviting despair. This means pointing your head in the direction you're already falling. You then experience, perhaps for the first time, the full brunt of the despair that you have been avoiding — despair from this lifetime and countless lifetimes, despair from your family, and despair from the entire world.

If you provide space for it, despair is always there for you to experience wherever you have avoided it. If you provide no space for the experience, it sinks out of sight, to persist subconsciously, awaiting the proper moment when you're willing to bear it.

In order to have space for despair, you have to be open and willing. You can't be distracted; you can't seek anything else. You need to be ready to get to the bottom of it — to discover for yourself what is real — by experiencing everything that is present on all levels, starting with what is just below the surface and going deeper.

When you experience despair fully, when you sink all the way in, you eventually fall out the bottom. Despair is not endless. You are. Falling through despair, you discover a black hole. All that stands between you and infinite nothingness is the ego's terror that it won't survive.

Your willingness to die to everything that is not real allows you to fall into the black hole. When you do, you discover a taste of your true Self, your soul. You realize directly the secret of emptiness, which is your true essence.

the recovery of essence

This recovery of essence can then flood the cellular memory of past wounds with love. All wounds heal in the presence of this nectar of love.

All wounds are valuable, for each wound contains a lesson for the ego to face. Analyzing, figuring it out, understanding your situation — all of these can be useful at a certain stage. Ultimately, however, what is required is your willingness to bear the wound and not run or defend. This is taking a stand in truth. Then all of your past wounding can come up for you to experience so you can finish with it once and for all.

When you act out of a motivation larger than personal egoic gain, you're taking a stand in the face of the ego's selfishness and defensiveness. This stand for what is natural and right, in the face of what is "normal" and demanded by egoic survival, deepens your commitment to the truth.

recovering essence through tests and challenges

You regain integrity and wholeness through your willingness to stay true while facing egoic challenges. For example, even though the egoic impulse for safety and security would dictate not speaking up, you can summon the courage, in the face of fear, to speak what is in your heart. Or, in the face of the lustful impulse to grab the next sweet temptation that comes along, you remain still, allowing the desire to burn and expose a deeper layer. In this way, you bring essence back into experience.

In the first example, you're staying true in the face of the mental fixation of fear; in the second, you're staying true in the face of the bodily fixation of lust. Deep integrity grows out of these acts of selflessness. However, when the ego tries to imitate staying true, a spiritual superego develops, with rules of conduct and other machinations of the mind.

All tests of the ego offer a similar challenge. You either stay true to selfishness, which is egoically based on fear and desire, or you stay true to selflessness, which is transcendentally based on your true nature as intelligent love.

Paradoxically, staying true can sometimes create ego inflation. The self-importance of having done the right thing inflates the ego's sense of itself, which shows up as arrogance and pride. This is simply the setup for the next test.

Let these tests come without resistance, and stay true no matter what arises. This is the only effective treatment for healing the wounding of the egoic sense of self.

CHAPTER TEN

the gatekeepers:
fear and doubt

Each day people arrive at the point where they could cross the road to freedom, only to turn back in fear because they see a dangerous snake lying in their way. They keep turning back when they see the snake until, one day, someone comes from the other side of the road at the same moment and tells them, "It's not a snake, only a rope." The snake did not have to be killed or transformed to make it safe to cross. It was always just a rope. Through the insight and guidance of someone who has already crossed to the other side, the seekers are able to see it as it really is.

The tests on the way back home from enslavement include facing your internal snakes, the prison gate-keepers of fear and doubt. Fear marks the borderline of ego. What you identify as "me" is inside the border, while what is outside is unknown and scary. Remember, since ego is a survival machine, all of its programs run to help you avoid fear and danger, and to stay safe and secure. Fear of the unknown keeps people shallow, involved only with trivialities, in an attempt to avoid the larger terror looming beneath the surface of things. The soul calls on you to stop engaging in your survival routines, and to stand and face the terror that has been running your life.

You avoid fear by thinking, and your thinking plays out the themes of doubt and security. Each time you have a thought that is based on a doubt or an attempt at security, you're avoiding the direct experience of fear. Uncertainty, caution, comparison, comment, internal discussion, disassociation, judgment, and chasing after the thought "What should I do?" are all neurotic ways to avoid the direct experience of the terror of the unknown.

varieties of fear

Although most fear is neurotic, in its pure form, fear can be wholesome. Wholesome fear is not mental, and is free of doubt. True fear is clean and leaves no aftertaste. You experience no hesitation in the moment. You take clear action without doubt, such as jumping back from an oncoming bus. There is no neurotic conversation in your mind about what to do, and no need to continue focusing on the fear after the moment has passed.

True wisdom reveals everything naturally. If there is reason for caution, it shows itself organically, not through your doubting mind. You smell it, taste it, and feel it — beyond any doubt.

Tension in the belly is a signal of neurotic fear caused by avoidance. The sense of tightening in your belly is caused by your unwillingness to feel the tension as an emotion. Fear comes first as a whisper, a soft rustling. If you don't listen to it, if you make believe it isn't there, it turns into a rattle. If you still ignore it, it becomes a shaking. If you persist in ignoring it even longer, it turns into a storm. And if you still continue to ignore it, it grabs you by the throat and doesn't let go until you pay attention.

Simply drop deeper than the mental mind, which is always talking to itself above the neck, and fall into the fear in the emotional body, as if you were falling into a well. It may seem like a gigantic ocean of fear, but sink even deeper. Feel the core of this solid, frozen terror, this iceberg of horror — something that you never wanted to feel.

The walls of your prison are made of fear — fear of what may lie on the other side. When you're finally finished with prison, it no longer makes a difference whether you're afraid or not. The walls of fear can no longer stop you.

doubt

When you're identified as your mind, you continue to have doubts. You wonder what is trustworthy. Out of this noise in your head, you experience confusion and lack of clarity. You're unable to see what is right in front of you because you're living in the past and the future, mentally disassociated from the present.

Because the egoic mind has taken the place of God, out of its arrogance it thinks of itself as the creator. If you're willing to abandon this arrogance of egoic inflation, then the mind surrenders and allows the heart to have control. Not the body, not the emotions, not the thoughts but the true heart — absolute silence, ever present; conscious love. Will immortal, conscious love be in control, or will your mind? That is the choice.

Doubt is fixation, and fixation is conditioned ego. As long as you believe that doubt has anything to teach you, you defend and deepen the fixation. Doubt is a general disease of the mind, the mental fear of falling into the unknown. When indulged to the extreme, doubt devolves into paranoia and mental instability.

Perhaps you have an experience of truth, of the groundlessness of pure being, and then fear arises. Out of fear comes doubt. With the doubt comes the story. From the story comes defense. And out of defense comes projection. Through this projection, you feel betrayed by some "other." Because you feel betrayed, you assume a false independence. You begin to put your trust in the doubt, wondering what to do, as the whole mad cycle of mind continues spinning. Your whole life has been a search for the divine. But, now that you've found what you've been looking for, you want to run away because you're afraid of being annihilated by love.

You may obsess on the question "What should I do?" to avoid the fear of annihilation. You are hanging on to your mind so you won't fall into fear, but in doing so, you're not present in the moment. If you're willing to invite the fear in, then it loses its power over you. Cut the connection to the thought of what the fear could mean and to the thought "What should I do?" If you're willing to experience the fear itself, you can discover that it leads you into the limitless beyond. It is really your own *shakti,* your own life force, leading you into emptiness. It lets you fall inside yourself, revealing the vastness therein.

Natural intuition speaks in silence. If you're talking to yourself, you can't hear intuition. Talking to yourself drains your life force. If doubt arises, do not follow it, and do not take it personally. It has nothing to teach you. It is just another passing thought. Anxiety and doubt are simply fear plus a story. If you stay in the story, you have no access to the fear.

Put the story aside. Stop engaging in doubt, and face everything. Invite the fear, let it get even stronger, and follow your heart.

Who you truly are can deal with everything. Who you *think* you are does not exist, so there is nothing to lose. When the person you think you are seems to dissolve, in keeping still you can realize who you really are.

What remains when you dissolve? What remains if you bear what you think is unbearable?

Your doubts are like a shot of heroin. You're addicted to them, and you think you need another shot. But these shots have nothing new to give you, nothing fresh. Stop. Give up your addictions. Your drugs are fear, doubt, and security. Don't touch them; they are poison.

fear of death

Often people report that they are happy when they are alone in nature, because there are no outside stimulators, so "I" remains dormant. But as soon as there is some risk, some danger, some other person, or something that the "I" has to do, it emerges to the foreground, and with it comes a thought, or usually many thoughts. This "I" is what you need to investigate, to see if it is real. Identifying yourself as this "I" is exhausting. It doesn't even allow you to be a very good worker. In fact, your job would run much more smoothly if this "I" didn't show up. What a relief it would be if there weren't this somebody constantly thinking about what needs to be done, how to do it properly, and reciting all the stories that go along with your particular movie!

The only purpose this "I" serves is to help you avoid the fear of death. But if you really want to be free, you're going to have to face death, and even welcome it. I am not talking here about the suicidal urge — the wish to die as a way of going back to sleep. It's not the body that has to die. Let the body live, and bear the unbearableness of being alive. If you bear it, it leads you to the inner abyss. Once you get to the abyss, there is nothing more to bear. Leave your entire burden behind, and fall into that abyss. It takes great courage to be willing to live, and at the same time to be willing to die, if that's what it takes to directly realize and serve the truth.

fear of madness

When you're avoiding the fear of death, you may feel as if you're going crazy. You enter into a fear of losing your mind. The very structure of your ego causes you to be terrified of madness as well as death. You fear losing control and sinking into delusion. But this is your current condition! You're out of control and talking to yourself right now; you're deluded right now.

Waking up isn't about becoming stupid, going mad, or running amok. You're already doing a fine job of that. What you're called upon to do is become sane — perhaps for the first time to see things as they are, free of projection. This is a move toward true sanity, but to the neurotic ego it seems like a loss of something.

When you're experiencing a fear of going mad, meet it fully. It can only arise as a voice in your head, talking to you. That voice *is* the madness. Be still, and stop following the voice of madness parading as a rational, intelligent, doubting Thomas. Drop into the fear located below your head. The wave of terror you haven't yet

experienced generates that voice and its story. By following the voice, you avoid the experience of direct terror.
If you're willing to meet the terror fully and directly, you
arrive at the deeper fear of annihilation.

Go directly into the fear. Invite it all in to be experienced. Fear from all your lifetimes, fear from your
family, fear from your culture — the fears of the entire
world and all its kingdoms are waiting for you to experience them. They point the way to the treasure that is
buried beneath.

facing death directly

The great Indian saint and sage Ramana Maharshi is
one of the most universally recognized enlightened
beings of our modern era. His awakening happened
quite spontaneously when he was sixteen years old. His
father had died the year before, and his family had
broken apart, with his mother and some children going
to one relative while he and a brother went to another.

Looking at it from our contemporary Western perspective, we can speculate that his father's death caused
a serious psychological dislocation for the boy. However
it may be, without any apparent external cause, one day
the boy became overwhelmed with the fear of death. He
decided to find out who dies, and he lay down on the
floor with his eyes closed to experience death. He fell
inside and realized that when the body dies, he does not
die. He realized that he is the deathless spirit that

inhabits a body. Shortly afterward, the boy lost interest in school and ran away from home to find his beloved holy mountain, Arunachala. Ramana Maharshi never left the mountain's side for the rest of his life. Thousands made their way from around the world to find him and sit in the presence of his blissful, loving, silent being.

In meeting fear directly, you see that it has no cause. When you meet the fear of death head-on, nothing dies except your ideas of yourself. The only thing that passes away is your identification as flesh. It isn't so much that it dies but that you see at last that it is insubstantial, without weight, having never really existed. It was all a case of mistaken identity! Ramana Maharshi's central teaching is that you are already the Self you are searching for. Anything that can be gained will be lost, he said. Find what does not come and go, and you will realize yourself as the immortal Self.

Of course facing death is terrifying. If it were not, this book would not be necessary. Nevertheless, you want to be free in spite of the fear. This doesn't mean waiting for the fear to leave — you stay true in the midst of fear. Walk through the fear of death, and discover that which does not die. Be fearless. Fear will arise, but your maturity lies in your willingness to meet the fear directly. None of your strategies for avoiding the fear work, whether you attempt to calm the mind, repress the fear, or change your circumstances. Even if you change your job or your relationships or your location, the fearful "I" still shows up.

Fear of death keeps you in bondage on the deepest level. It keeps you enslaved. This is what makes freedom so rare. You can't just shop online to buy freedom. Nor can you find freedom in some faraway adventure. You find freedom in the willingness to turn around and face the fear of death, to meet it directly, here and now. Better to be free with a dead body than to be a slave in a sleepwalking nightmare called life. This realization is the beginning of a beautiful flowering.

Your body isn't the problem. The problem is the unexamined belief that there is a *somebody* in control of this body. This idea of a *somebody* has to come face-to-face with its own death.

Then you find out what doesn't die. When you realize yourself to be that which does not die, you experience the body as a great gift and a holy incarnation. It is indeed precious, but it isn't who you are. If you worship the body without first meeting the fear of death, then you identify yourself as a body, and you defend the body at the cost of liberation and true freedom.

If all you want is for the fear of death to go away, you miss a great opportunity. There are many ways to separate yourself from fear. A whole pharmacopoeia is available to help you suppress fear. Many people prefer to narcotize their fears. They are satisfied with their sleep being comfortable enough that they never have to feel the fear of death. When they get a whiff of their mortality, their tendency is to get a prescription for an antidepressant or a tranquilizer.

We have inherited a deep-rooted genetic and family-conditioned fear that the body could die from starvation, from cancer, from unforeseen calamity. The body is going to die — that much is certain. On an egoic level, you either deny this reality or you're terrified of it. If you're willing to invite the fear of death in and say, "Okay, death, come and get me," you cut through identification with the body. By facing the fear of death directly, and by being willing to die for the truth, you cross over to the other side. You realize directly that which does not die.

Typically, *everything* in your life is run by the fear of death. You may have spiritual reasons for everything you're doing, but underneath all of that lies this uninvestigated fear. You're very lucky to have this fear. Make good use of it! Invite it to get stronger. Say to yourself, "It's a good day to die. I am committed to finding the truth. Truth is more important than fear."

When fear arises, feel it totally. At some point it will leave and something else will take its place. Feel this something else fully, and it, too, will pass. Everything comes and everything goes, except that which you are. Events and experiences come and go, but *you* are always here. Consciousness is always here.

Fear is the secret gateway in. Discover that which

doesn't die. Rest in that. This is the beginning of life. Once fear no longer has a meaning, you can meet it without a story. Then you will probably notice that what you once called fear was actually a flash of vitality.

In the same light, be willing to be insecure. In your insecurity, you discover true security. All of your mental activity and imagination never give you security. They give you a life of slavery based on an idea of security.

Surrender to the divine. Let everything come up. To be healthy means to be in the present moment. To be in the present moment means to experience everything and fall deeper. What dissolves is suffering. What remains is the purity of love that is your true Self.

PART FOUR

AWAKENING

grace, awakening, and silence

It is time to wake up. You have received the call. You have gathered the courage to follow it. You have devoted yourself to freedom. You have experienced tastes of your true Self. Now it is time to rest.

the supreme yoga of rest

Once you have done all that you can do — having gathered all of your intention and resources to the one burning issue of freedom; having left all concepts and knowing behind; having given up your control, contraction, and defense; having faced the terror of death and having invited everything to come in — then your job is finished. Then you can rest.

Rest is the supreme yoga. The ego misunderstands and abuses the idea of rest by thinking of it as laziness or loss of focus. Rest is not lazy. Rest is clear, focused, and present. Rest can be very active, but there is no stress, no effort, no distraction, no impatience, and no wait-ing. True rest is alert, relaxed, and open.

The art of not moving is the fulfillment of the supreme yoga of rest. Calling this condition of not moving rest is perhaps misleading, as it is hot, intense, and often emotionally painful. Many people mistake rest for comfort, but this kind of rest may not be com-fortable. Rather, it allows discomfort to come and burn in the fire of freedom. Rest in non-movement is the ever-alert clarity of intelligence, inviting the pain of all identifications to come and burn in the fire of love, fueled by the hurricane of silence.

True rest reveals silence, and silence is the song of God. It is the ever-overflowing fullness of emptiness. Then, grace appears.

grace

Grace is one of the faces of love, and love is your true Self.

The word *love,* like the word *God,* has become pol-luted through misuse. Love is not an idea left over from your past conditioning. It is not about a "somebody" loving a "somebody else." Many languages have a range of words for love. Persian has over ten different words, such as words for the love between a mother and child, the love between a father and son, the love between sis-ters, and the love between secret lovers. The supreme love, however, is the true love of the heart, surrendering from one side and embracing itself from the other.

Many have heard this and have conceptualized love to be passive. But love is in no way passive. Love is the active force of emptiness.

Love appears in many guises depending on the role.

As the initiator of the ego/soul, love appears first as death, the fearsome guardian at the gates of immortality.

Once the ego/soul has consciously faced death, then love appears as grace to take the soul back to the other side. In a moment of grace, you drop the ego as a butterfly drops the cocoon. What is left is the liberated soul incarnate in form.

The ego can't force grace, for love does not serve the ego. The ego can't earn grace, for not one of us has earned the grace of awakening. The ego can't manipulate or control grace. Only in surrendering all control can the ego invite grace. It is terrifying to give up control. In the life of an animal, control is an evolutionary advantage. You can't surrender control if you don't first face the illusion that you're in control. Then and only then can grace enter.

Grace, however, is no magical elixir that changes events and stops pain. Horrors do happen on Earth. Good people die senselessly, while horrible murderers live out their lives in comfort and wealth. Grace does not change these horrors.

What grace does is more mysterious. Grace allows good use to be made of the horror and senseless brutality. Grace transforms unconscious suffering into conscious suffering. The ego runs from suffering and suffers all the more. Grace allows you to stop running and meet pain directly. In this way, suffering as you knew it ends. Now the conscious bearing of suffering — personal, relational, global, and universal — evokes the bliss of surrender and the joy of gratitude, which is the natural response of the open heart to the grace of revelation. Revelation is the fruit of bearing the pain because pain is the secret gateway into your Self. Grace is the mysterious divine force that takes you across the ocean of suffering while you remain in the midst of the horror of the world.

Then you face a choice. Your life can be given back to grace, where it serves to end the suffering in the world. This is a task similar to emptying the ocean with a teacup, but it is the holy work of grace. In it, the bliss of surrender ever deepens. You find the joy, love, and goodness that is present everywhere, and the nectar of immortality nourishes you.

You then realize that there is no one serving, no one being served, and no act of service. This realization opens another hole in the ground of being, and you realize your true Buddha nature. Then the Buddha surrenders its seat and picks up the cup and returns to emptying the sea of suffering.

being your self

"Just be natural! Be yourself!" mothers often say to their children.

But what does this really mean? All of our lives we have tried different strategies for being ourselves. For some of us, being ourselves means acting out our lusts and fantasies. For others of us, being ourselves means doing what we think is expected from the outside.

The truth is, you can't *be* yourself until you *know* yourself. Realization is the fruit of surrender. The depth of bliss signals the depth of surrender into your Self. Surrender invites grace, and grace bestows realization of the truth.

When you know who you truly are, when you have passed through the gateway of death and drowned in the nectar of immortality, you know yourself unshakably, beyond doubt or reason. This knowing transcends all knowledge.

With this knowing, you are established in the realization of your Self. You can't reach this level of realization without a period of intense burning in the fire of not moving. The fire of not moving in the face of all temptation burns up latent identification.

Latent thoughts of pride and specialness arise with the realization of divinity. To give the pride and specialness a second thought is the trap of the egoic mind. If you don't touch it — and by touch it, I mean following it as if it were real — it ignites in a holy flame of love that reveals a depth beyond what you had realized a moment before. Soon you see that what had seemed so deep, and in fact was so deep in comparison with the rest of your life, is but the shallow ledge of a deeper ocean. Then the bottom drops out, and you are one.

awakening

Many people have heard wondrous reports of the moment of enlightenment. It is a moment that can't be described with words, because enlightened beings receive a knowledge that is beyond all knowledge.

All that can be said is that everything you thought was real is revealed to be insubstantial, and you realize reality as the permanent condition of your Self.

The great trap is that people chase the experience of enlightenment, which is a by-product of realization. Chasing the enlightenment experience is like chasing the smoke that is a by-product of fire, and missing the fire itself. You cannot successfully chase an experience of enlightenment. *That* is the ego trying to do the job of grace. All you can do is surrender.

While some people chase enlightenment too hard, others give up on enlightenment too easily, assuming it is not real. Freud claimed to have never had an oceanic experience of oneness and so theorized that it was an infantile egoic experience that some people remember from the past. Others feel that there is nothing they can do to wake up, and so instead they try simply to "be here now."

This is missing the point in the other direction. Giving up and accepting yourself just as you are can function as an egoic trap of either resignation or indulgence. When you're truly present in the moment, your inner life alters on the most fundamental level.

The experience of awakening is essential, and it is completely personal. It isn't the experience that you have read about or imagined. You have your own unique experience of awakening, because it is reflected through your particular mind's eye.

Each incarnation comprises a genetic blueprint that is different from every other being on Earth. Each has a unique point of view in relative time and space. No other being occupies, has occupied, or will occupy your particular moment.

Thus, the revelation of the one cosmic being is unique to you. There is not just one experience of awakening but countless experiences of oneness — some deeper, some wider, some very short and shallow.

Since grace is your own heart calling you home, grace prepares the way in exactly the right form for your mind and circumstances. There are usually many glimpses that lead up to awakening, as the mind's eye blinks open and shut. Most people receive many tastes of the range of divine flavors before the final stopping of mind.

This stopping reveals that which is behind all experience. The supreme *sahaj samadhi* — completely being your Self in the face of all states — establishes itself in human form.

Each time you touch the unknown, you come away with a deeper appreciation of its vastness and its diversity. This is similar to touching a few square inches of an elephant's knee. Besides feeling the texture of the skin, the folds and lines, you're aware that there is a much larger presence. Self is the formless, timeless totality of consciousness, taking all forms, faces, and roles as it wakes up to itself and marvels at its own reflection in countless unique lives.

after enlightenment

People often expect that their lives will change radically once they have awakened. The ego searches for enlightenment, so egoic ideas of what it will be like are projections from the past. In truth, there is no way of knowing how your life will appear. You may believe that all of your problems will disappear. It is more likely that all of your problems will persist, but as allies. They will be useful in helping you discover the structures of your own mind as your realization deepens.

Many believe that enlightenment cures the illnesses of the body. This isn't necessarily so! What it heals is your relationship to the illnesses of the body. If you eat poorly and neglect your oral hygiene, eventually your teeth decay. Changing your diet and improving your hygiene does not restore the teeth that have already decayed and fallen out. This is simply the karma of the situation.

The body is the repository of all past karmic momentum. Everything leaves its trace. If you're awake, nothing is a problem for you. Even the body slowly rotting and decaying back toward its inevitable decline and death is not a problem. Everything is useful, and nothing needs to be different. With this awareness, you live a life of happiness and peace even in the midst of your karmic arisings.

Someone once asked Ramana Maharshi why his body was deformed from his long sitting, so that he had facial tics and needed to use a walking stick. He replied, "Once the elephant enters the tent, the tent is never the same."

Many believe that once they are enlightened, they will become great teachers. This may be so, although being a teacher may take a different form than the one you expect. Indeed, nothing may change on the outside, but those who are enlightened radiate peace, love, and silence, so that lucky souls who are ripe catch it from them. This starts with your immediate relationships — not through preaching, teaching, correcting, or pointing out errors, but rather through the silent emanation of love that is kind, supportive, clean, and honest, with no vested interest in the outcome.

Some are afraid that if they become enlightened they will end up like Ramana Maharshi, living alone on a mountain with no possessions. If this is indeed your destiny, it will find you without a conscious decision, and you will experience it as bliss beyond measure. More likely your life will continue rolling along in the groove it is already in. This in itself is the teaching of rest. Don't force anything, don't avoid anything, and don't land anywhere. In this way, you discover the natural joy of being yourself.

silence

After you have become established in your true Self, thoughts come and go with no consequence. Useful thinking is useful, fanciful thinking is fanciful, and you see the old dysfunctional neurotic preoccupations for what they are and leave them untouched, to be swallowed back into silence.

Silence is the ground of being; a well without a bottom, sides, or boundaries. When you are silent, things take care of themselves. In true silence, there is clarity and intelligence. You're able to see things as they are, and true wisdom and right action appear quite naturally.

Another word for silence is reality. As long as you believe what you see is real, what you think is real, and what you feel is real, you miss out on reality. Reality is invisible and ever present. When you discover silence, you discover its inherent reality. Reality means "that which doesn't change, that which doesn't come and go, that which doesn't end." When you truly know this, you can discriminate between what is real and what is unreal, and live in reality instead of projection, which is the mind's idea of reality projected onto what is perceived as outside yourself.

While all experiences are subjective, the constant is objective silence. Silence is not about the absence of noise. Silence is the ground in which both noise and quiet appear. In order for you to penetrate the truth of silence, the noise of the mind has to stop for a period of time.

This stopping of the mind is one of the universal hallmarks of grace. Whatever realizations occur, the stopping of the flow of thoughts is essential. Otherwise, you conceptualize all realizations as soon as the moment passes. If you're practicing the supreme yoga of rest, after grace stops the mind you are vigilant in not picking up the next thought. You see the thought start to rise like a bubble out of emptiness, but you don't touch it no matter how great the temptation. This is your response to grace.

If you meet grace with the open, clear vigilance that does not touch any thought at all, then silence deepens beyond measure, and you experience a deeper union as the mind is reabsorbed back into the soul, and the soul is reabsorbed back into its source. Silence then reveals the deeper realms of emptiness hidden by the veils of mind.

What makes this realization stable is silence and the discipline of mind. Within the discipline of the supreme yoga of rest, you encounter many experiences, but they are passing. What endures is a sense of abiding love.

For what is silence other than love?

CHAPTER TWELVE

transmission:
the gift of the teacher

When grace appears from within, it pulls you into its depths. For the ripest souls, this is all that is needed, and awakening is instantaneous. Ramana Maharshi and the seminal Zen master Hui Neng are perfect examples of these ripest of souls.

Hui Neng was an illiterate woodcutter in seventh-century China. One day while delivering a load of wood, he overheard a recitation of the Buddhist Diamond Sutra, and he woke up. He then went to find his master, who sent him to the kitchen to pound rice. When his realization ripened after many years in the kitchen, he received the transmission of his master. He became the Sixth Zen Patriarch, and the founder of the School of Sudden Awakening in southern China.

the teacher: grace in form

For most of us, however, the call from within isn't enough. We need grace to appear in form as well as from within. When grace appears from without, it takes the form of the true teacher. The true teacher is the living transmission who reveals the most intimate depths of the vastness of Self.

In Sanskrit, the word for teacher is *guru.* There are many kinds of gurus or teachers. But the final teacher is the *sat-guru,* the living transmission of immortal being. The sat-guru is the sword that swings the final cut in the process of awakening.

The sat-guru is the black hole of totality that you finally surrender to, at the end of the long road of the spiritual path. All the other teachers were important, preparing you, testing you, pointing you in the right direction, but then each sits down beside the road while you proceed on to the end. Where the road ends, where the universe ends, the sat-guru awaits, welcoming you with open arms and eyes of fire. The sat-guru then declares the final truth that there is no path, no journey, and no one going anywhere. Since these words are infused with the living realization of truth, they penetrate directly to the heart of the ripe soul of the seeker ready to stop the seeking. Everything bursts into light as the inner soul is kindled and burns bright in response to the sat-guru's confirmation.

The sat-guru is the embodiment of the divine principle in human form, the ultimate confirmation that reality is real, and that everything that we typically call "reality" is an illusion. After passing on the flame of awakening, the sat-guru is there to keep tossing the burning wood back into the fire, so that nothing escapes unburned.

The sat-guru is your own Self, looking back at you through a fleshly form, confirming you as silent immortal love. When your heart appears in a human form, it transmits the living openness that is your own possibility. This teacher is your own true Self, transmitting the possibility of freedom.

the teacher's role

A teacher is of great importance in showing you the reflection of yourself so that you can see your Self clearly, so that you can recognize the truth of the situation. This is the confirmation that is required. It is also the guard against the inevitable ego inflation that occurs if you believe that you did it yourself. You have to be both willing to do it yourself, and to surrender completely to the grace that is the help. Sitting in the presence of awakened consciousness, there is a transmission of silence. This is the teacher's grace that naturally silences the mind, so that seeing can be clear and direct.

Papaji said, "There is only one teacher. It is alive in your heart. It speaks to you in silence. If you're not able to understand the language of silence, it is because you're too busy talking to yourself and making too much noise in your head. Then the teacher from within your own heart appears in front of you in a human form to speak to you in your own lisping tongue. This teacher says to you, 'Yes, you!'"

avoiding the consumer trap

These days it seems that everyone knows about the damage false teachers can cause. We have all seen or heard about teachers who have abused power by manipulating their followers emotionally, sexually, or financially. When someone once asked my teacher, Papaji, why there were so many false teachers, he replied, "Because there are so many false seekers, and everyone needs a teacher." He also said, "As long as there are sheep, there will be shepherds. You can't herd lions. If you're acting like a sheep, don't blame the shepherd!"

Those who awaken without a teacher avoid the consumer trap, but they can fall into an even greater trap, which is the egoic idea that they "did it." Those who don't find a teacher, or who leave a teacher prematurely, often fall back into delusion as an "enlightened somebody special."

In our consumer age, the tendency is to rush to see whatever teacher happens to be in town, and then to go again when the next one passes through. This results in an endless cycle of temporary highs and crashes, with endless discussions of spiritual concepts. Shopping around from teacher to teacher is a way of avoiding commitment to the real work at hand. Consider how ineffective therapy would be if you went to a different psychotherapist every week! Similarly, establishment in your true nature is quite difficult, if not impossible, unless you're willing to stay with one teacher until the process is complete. Often the ego escapes the death grip of the teacher by leaving too soon, usually with an inflated spiritual story, or a story of the teacher's shortcomings to rationalize turning away.

If you get caught up in the trap of chasing enlightenment, you're just pursuing another illusion. Chasing promising descriptions of teachers only leads you to another movie, another distraction from reality. The tendency of our modern culture is to taste a little bit of this and a little bit of that — a little high here, and another experience there.

Eventually, you're finished with seeking new experiences. At that moment, if you're lucky, you meet with something altogether different. Not just another experience, not just another beautiful vision, not just another Tantric high, not just another spiritual journey, but something so deep that it stops you right in your tracks. You're finished with window-shopping, and your whole attention turns within.

finding the true teacher

If you stay true to your innermost being, a true teacher appears exactly when needed. Everything is taken care of perfectly. Your own Self appears to welcome you home. The Self knows what you need much better than you do. You can trust the love that is calling you deeper. You can trust this fire that burns everything.

When you find the true teacher, don't move, no matter what. Most people are terrified of what true commitment might mean. Often they stay through the honeymoon period, when all is ecstasy, and then, when things start to get uncomfortable for the egoic mind, when the experience starts to feel deep and hot, or dead and boring, fears arise. Along with discomfort comes the tendency to look for a new teacher with whom to have a fresh romance.

The call for the final teacher is crucial. If you call for the final teacher and something true shows up, you know it is real beyond doubt. Through the grace of transmission, you have a direct experience of truth. But then a response has to come from your side as well; otherwise, this experience won't have a lasting effect. The spiritual philosopher/teacher Gurdjieff would say it is a shock that temporarily throws you into a higher orbit, only to decay and fall back in on itself. In this manner, a touch of grace leads to the arising of the latent subconscious identity as special, which is ego inflation. Without a response from your side, the inflation continues and essence is lost.

If you really want freedom above all else, then you're willing and available to respond. Responding means devoting yourself completely to truth and love.

Many people experienced the transmission of the great Indian saint and fully realized sat-guru Ramana Maharshi. Thousands of people traveled to see him, but only a handful woke up. Those who woke up were the ripe ones who responded with love and intelligence. Not only did they feel the grace of transmission that drowned them in bliss, but they also responded by giving their hearts and using the clarity of their wisdom to see through illusion and devote themselves to the truth.

My teacher, Papaji, would say that the bird of freedom flies with two wings: inquiry and devotion. This was his way of naming the two faces of intelligent love.

tests of commitment

Your response to grace meets with tests. What you've said you're willing to give for freedom returns to haunt you, to pull you back into your past. As you awaken, you eventually confront the fear of death, as I described in chapter 10. This is a gift of the teacher. You come face-to-face with the terrible fear of annihilation, which is the gateway in. When you pass this gateway, like Ramana Maharshi you discover that which doesn't die. When your life is offered in surrender, you realize immortal intelligent life as your true nature.

surrender

What is often called surrender isn't true surrender but instead a giving up. This giving up comes with a sense of "I can't do it anymore. I'm going to let you do it for me." This is very different from true surrender. Giving up has to do with control, but now you're giving up control to another to tell you what to do.

When people tell me they have surrendered to false teachers, I usually find that this means they have given up responsibility by handing over their authority to someone else. Now "the other" has authority. This is simply a form of looking for a better parent who will finally tell you what to do, tell you how to do it, protect you, affirm that you're a good boy or girl, and tell you that you have done it right and now you get to be the favorite.

A true teacher is not concerned with running your private life. If you are looking for someone to tell you to marry or divorce, have sex or abstain, work here or there, do this or that, you are looking for an authority to successfully guide your personal life. But your personal life is not the teacher's concern. What you do or how you act is always a by-product of realization or ignorance. The teacher is only interested in your liberation from the false identity that takes everything personally.

Genuine surrender to a true teacher is very rare because this is the most mature of relationships. The true teacher sees that you already are what you're seeking. This teacher sees that there is no fundamental difference between you and the teacher. The true teacher wants only your awakening: to see the same reality that the teacher sees.

The true teacher *is* the perfect parent, but this is just a by-product. If you're searching for a perfect parent, you're searching for a shepherd. In this case, as the words of Papaji suggest, you find yourself in a flock and wonder why the shepherd betrayed you. But only sheep show up with shepherds. The shepherd usually takes the position of being above the sheep and different from the sheep. The shepherd considers himself divine, and lets the sheep know they are lucky to have him around. The shepherd does not bestow freedom, but rather a sense of security and belonging.

A true teacher does not tell you what to do or not do with your life. This teacher does not say, "Quit your job and follow me." A true teacher isn't concerned with your daily activities. That is your business. A true teacher is concerned only with your liberation, and this has nothing to do with form or activities.

A true teacher knows teaching is just a role and there is no fundamental difference between the one playing the seeker and the one playing the teacher. A true teacher is quite happy to drop the role and play something else as the moment dictates.

falling in love with the teacher

Sometimes people ask me whether it's unwise to be attached to anything, even a true teacher. Isn't it strange, when you consider all the attachments in your life — people you aren't willing to face or to leave — that the one you're most afraid of, the one you're most willing to drop, is the one who can set you free?

I fell in love with my teacher. And in this falling in love, my willingness deepened. By falling in love I do not mean a romantic love, although the excitement of that energy was included as well. It was not a desire or longing for something lacking in the moment, as is often the case with romantic love, which needs expression, reciprocation, and consummation. When I fell into the love that *is* my teacher, there was no need for anything to be different from the way it was. The perfection of the moment was so overwhelming that nothing extra could be added.

True love is something that does not come and go. Such love is your very nature. However, attachments are sure to come and go. Attachments support the neurotic ideas you have of yourself. If you need to be attached to anything at all, be attached to true love. By true love, I don't mean the love for an object. Mostly, when we speak of love, we mean the love for objects. You love these objects because they evoke particular feelings. What people call love is all too commonly selfishness: "I love you as long as you make me feel good. If you don't make me feel good, then I don't love you anymore." Of course, people are rarely honest enough to state this dynamic so blatantly. Instead, they fabricate elaborate stories of leverage and betrayal.

The last attachment to go is love for the true teacher. This is the attachment to the true beloved. As long as this body lasts, the love for my teacher will remain. Because it is a true love affair, if you never leave the true teacher, the teacher never leaves you. There is a meeting in silence that is the melding of two souls. There is love meeting love endlessly.

In the end, what is left — you or the teacher? If you abandon the teacher, you yourself are left. Lose your attachment to your identity instead. If you leave all ideas of yourself, only the true teacher remains. Then you and the teacher are one, and this is bliss.

CHAPTER THIRTEEN

who you really are

The most important question we can ask is "Who am I?" If you ask this question on the deepest level, if you stick with it, moving beyond the superficial answers of your name, occupation, relationship status, and other forms of ego identification, you enter the depths of the unknown. There you find yourself.

A great trap is to stop with the concept of no-self. Some people tend to say that there is no one here to answer the question "Who am I?" What a good joke. The one who says there is no one here is the one who searches within for the true answer that is beyond mind!

There is no life without consciousness. There is no intelligence without consciousness. There is no one to ask this question without consciousness. *You* are consciousness.

If consciousness imagines itself to be a thinking

somebody who imagines that there is no one to ask the question, this thinking somebody can also turn around to find out who he or she is.

Is there really a thinking somebody who turns around? No. Yet, to claim that there is no one asking the question implies that you have not grasped the essential. If you're asking the question "Who is there to ask?" *you* are the one.

In this chapter, I share with you a dialogue between me, wearing the guise of the teacher, and Ellen, a young woman who came as a seeker to one of my meetings. This dialogue shows the moment of opening to the recognition of the true Self. Who you really are is here, now.

identification

ELLEN: You commonly use the term *identification,* and I'm not sure what you mean. Can you explain?

ELI: What's your name?

ELLEN: Ellen.

ELI: There it is. That's what I mean!

[Ellen starts laughing, and enormous laughter fills the room and continues for several minutes as everyone catches it. It builds in waves, recedes, and builds again.]

ELLEN: Okay, I get it.

ELI: Yes. Now, "Ellen" disappeared for an instant. What is left? In that moment, there is no past, no future, nothing to see, nothing to think about, no voices in your head, no "Ellen." What is left?

ELLEN: Just tranquility and relief.

ELI: Yes, tranquility and relief.

ELLEN: It's a big burden carrying "Ellen" around.

ELI: That's right. "Ellen" is a self-inflicted wound.

[Ellen bursts into laughter again.]

ELLEN: Wow! You're right!!

[More laughter as everyone catches it.]

ELI: Yes. What a relief — instant healing! Because in that healing, there is suddenly no need for everyone else to bandage and care for the wound. It doesn't have to ooze.

ELLEN: *[still laughing]* I probably spend ninety-nine percent of my time maintaining, supporting, and bandaging.

ELI: Yes, that's it — free time! Really good news! Then there's no more "Ellen." The wound is healed. Life is perfect just as it is. You're happy, fulfilled. Then your life becomes a life of peace and love and tranquility.

ELLEN: So the identification is the trap?

ELI: That's right. With no belief in "Ellen," no one suffers.

ELLEN: Is that what you mean by "taking it personally"?

ELI: That's right, taking it personally is "Ellen." "Ellen" takes everything personally.

ELLEN: *[laughing]* You obviously know her.

ELI: Yes, the relief immediately spreads to everyone around you.

ELLEN: This identification seems to be a common affliction.

ELI: That's right; it's a group trance. And the very people who are called your best friends are the ones who re-induce you into your trance so that they can stay in theirs. Best friends listen to your story of "Ellen" and believe it.

ELLEN: Yes, oh yes.

ELI: This is such good news. You have glimpsed the possibility of a lifetime of peace, tranquility, love, fulfill-ment, and happiness. What would your mother say if you called her and said, "I called to tell you I'm happy, I'm at peace"? "I love you and everything is forgiven," you tell her. "There's no problem anymore. My life is fulfilled." Oh, what a message! Who would believe it? This spacious, vast, unknown, empty, intelligent love is the truth of who you are. It's what you were so scared of.

ELLEN: Well, it doesn't sound scary when you put it that way.

the ego's fear

ELI: That's right; it's just scary to "Ellen" and her ideas, her beliefs.

ELLEN: So, it's the ego that's terrified of being discov-ered and disassembled.

ELI: That's right, because it knows it's not real.

ELLEN: Well, then, what is its purpose?

ELI: It's there so that you can wake up and see who you are. *[laughing]*

ELLEN: But that seems to be waking up to see who you are *not*.

ELI: That's right. That's exactly how it works. You see who you are not, in order to wake up from it.

ELLEN: On some level I have always known that's not who I am.

ELI: Exactly. The ego is terrified of being found out, because it knows it's a fraud. You've known it all along. Everyone does. Everyone knows it about you and about themselves, but they're willing to lie about it if you're willing to lie about it. Then you can go to self-esteem groups to learn how to feel really good about "Ellen."

Seeing through this identification is the way out of the prison, but most prisoners are terrified of getting out. Many go back to prison because of their terror of the unknown. In prison they have a routine, and even if they don't like it, it is known.

ELLEN: There's a familiar environment, familiar territory. You may not function well, but...

ELI: That's right. It may be hell, but...

ELLEN: ...it's *my* hell. *[laughing]*

ELI: And once you're out of prison, once you turn your back on "Ellen," you come to see, as you already know, that none of it ever really existed. There is no prison, there is no ego, and there is no "Ellen." It was all just a bad dream you've been living in.

ELLEN: But if I stop carrying "Ellen" around, all of those old habits and tricks are going to arise to try to trap me again and pull me back into being "Ellen."

the tests of buddha

ELI: That's right. Those are called the tests of the Buddha. Do you know the Buddha's story?

The Buddha was a prince who had everything in the world: parents who loved him, wives who loved him, consorts, dancing girls — all the luxuries the world could provide. But he wasn't satisfied, he wasn't happy. He had to leave it all behind. He had to leave his palace, his wives, his babies, and his whole life, to go off and find the true meaning of life.

He spent years trying everything until, finally, he said, "Okay, I've tried everything, and none of it has really worked. I'm going to sit under this tree right here until I realize the truth."

And he sat under that tree for days.

After days of sitting there, he woke up. He saw that none of it really existed, that it was all a dream. He realized himself as immortal consciousness, pristine emptiness. He realized that he had always been and always would be — that there's nothing else but this. Everything else is just an appearance, so that we can come to this realization.

Then, the Buddha was attacked by armies of demons. At least that is how these tests were depicted in more primitive times. As more modern folks, we might say that the dark side arose from the latent subconscious. The demons confronted him and said, "Who do you think you are? Who said you could sit under this tree? This isn't your tree. What are you doing here? Get out, now!"

This terror and all the other latent tendencies showed up as demons. But the Buddha didn't move, and when the demons threw their spears, they passed right through him because there was no one there to catch them.

Then some dancing girls showed up and said, "Oh, you've been sitting for so long, God doesn't want you to suffer. Come, let us give you a massage. We'll take care of you." *[laughter]*

when your tests show up

ELI: And as the latent identification called "Ellen," when your own tests — your own personal masseuse — show up, "you" will immediately want to say, "Yes, I've been waiting to be loved, to be cared for." But if you don't move, if you stay sitting under that tree, these tests disappear. And you realize you're already completely fulfilled. You need nothing from anywhere else. You are love itself. Then your heart of love overflows and you pass it on.

Like the Buddha, you know that there's really no one asleep and, in fact, this material existence doesn't really exist. It is just a dream; it's just empty space, vibrating, blinking. Through your heart of compassion, you pass on emptiness, silence, and love to whoever is interested. And if they're not interested, you don't bother them. You don't preach it.

Just be yourself. "Ellen" will continue to appear as a form, but now it is informed by the truth of your Self. Then, whatever the karma is, whatever your momentum of this life is — whether it is to be a mother, a lover, a wife, or whatever — it doesn't matter. That role plays itself empty and is filled with love, because there is no one to take it personally.

These tests have to come up to show you where you're still identified as "Ellen." They are very useful. It is useful for fear to come back. It is useful for attachment to arise again, to show you where there is still latent attachment. When you feel the pain of it, the unbearableness of it, it burns.

If you don't indulge it, and you don't repress it, and you don't lie about it — if you just feel it fully — it burns. Then a deeper bliss appears. Suddenly the bottom falls out of emptiness, and you fall into an ocean of love. It's been there all along. Who you really are is limitless.

realizing who you are

ELLEN: So by not resisting, I can move through all the tests of Buddha?

ELI: Yes. Not resisting means not moving at all, because if there is some belief that you still have to do something, then you move somewhere. But who you truly are is silent, immovable emptiness. No resistance means no barrier, no separation between you and the full experience of life.

ELLEN: So, it is "Ellen" who feels the terror.

ELI: "Ellen" *is* the terror. As long as there is some terror, there is some "Ellen." Consciousness experiences everything. Awareness is here when there is an "Ellen," and awareness is here when there is no "Ellen." You are the field of awareness that all states come and go in.

ELLEN: After our session yesterday, last night I woke up and I was terrified. I no longer knew if I had a body, or where my legs and arms were, until I touched them. Then images from my childhood suddenly appeared.

ELI: You woke up in a moment of clarity. You didn't know if you had a body. Very good report, if you stop here. But then you got scared, so you put yourself back together again. You touched the body to reassure yourself of your identity, and then you went back to sleep in a movie you call reality. The movie is based on your childhood and your need to talk about it. You feel certain in your belief that this is you.

Through grace, you were touched. You had a moment in which you did not know who you were. Everything after that was just reidentification with the dream. Come back to not knowing. It is always here. You had an excellent chance last night. What a moment of grace! Stay true to that. Don't sell yourself. Don't put yourself back together again. Remain free of any idea or sensation. Be still, and everything is revealed.

ELLEN: If I put "Ellen" down and cease carrying her

as this field of consciousness, are there still feelings of fear and terror?

ELI: Sure. Everything shows up. When you absolutely know the latent tendencies of mind for what they are, they burn away and eventually they don't show up because you have used them up. You're not fueling new ones, and you're not indulging in old ones. When the old ones arise, they burn, and this just adds fuel to the fire of freedom. If fear shows up, you welcome it, because it is showing you someplace where you're still identified as "Ellen." If you let the fear burn, you deepen in peace and happiness.

The egoic idea is to run away from pain and toward pleasure. And this leads to suffering, coming and going. When you're willing to stop indulging in the trance of "Ellen," you find that pain actually leads to the deepest bliss and pleasure. But you can't run from fear, and you can't chase it. You don't need it, and you don't need to not have it. Then there is no problem with fear. It's a gateway. It's a gift. If fear never arises, no problem. If fear always arises, no problem. Then there is nothing to grasp and nothing to push away, nothing to chase and nothing to resist.

ELLEN: Thank you so much. It is all very clear. All so beautifully simple.

ELI: You are very welcome. Yes, it is very clear.

CHAPTER FOURTEEN

the roar of awakening

The roar of awakening is a laugh. You laugh so hard, you fall over and can't breathe. You laugh at all the madness, all the false fronts, all the mistaken identities. You laugh and you cry at the same moment, both without cause and filled with cause. You laugh at God, you laugh at the world, and most of all, you laugh at yourself.

Awakening is realizing your true nature as immortal Self. This awakening happens suddenly after lifetimes of gradual ripening, just as a sweet fruit drops all of a sudden from the tree when its moment of ripeness comes, after beginning as a hard, bitter green bud.

Self-realization is a leap forward in the evolution of the species. It is the fulfillment of the process of individuation and the ultimate outcome of the stages of ego, as well as the return home as the one source of all. This return isn't about going backward. It's not about going back to sleep, or going back to the ignorance of the animal; rather, it's a return of individuated consciousness awake as universal consciousness.

True freedom means the realization of who you *already are*. This is not who you *will* be, not what you still have to work on, not something that you have to fix or transform, not something you have to create. The direct realization of who you are already, and who you have always been, is freedom from the bondage of misidentification.

the teacher as living embodiment

My teacher, Papaji, was the living embodiment of the wake-up call. Preparing you for some future awakening was not his function. Rather, he assumed that if you made it to him, you were already prepared, ripe, and ready. He welcomed all who found their way to his door, and he transmitted the final teaching. He said that simply having a human incarnation was sufficient qualification for directly realizing the truth of reality.

And this is the truth. You don't need a special kind of birth. You don't need to be a saint or an avatar. Self-realization is natural, arriving as the culmination of the long alienation of the ego.

If you're willing to be your true Self completely, what shows up is a mysterious unfolding of life. It won't be a *normal* life, but rather, a natural life.

In a normal life all your thoughts are about "I want

this, and I don't want that." The ego is always either trying to get something, or trying to keep something away. It is a defense against the outside world, as well as a defense against the depths of the inside. The egoic mind manages in a small bubble of space between the inner and outer, with fear guarding the borders.

the donkey and the lion

Papaji's favorite story, told to him by his mother when he was a young boy, provides a beautiful metaphor depicting "normal life" as the life of a donkey.*

Papaji told this story many times, to people who arrived in his living room from all over the world. Each time he told this story, it was as fresh as the first time, with each telling bringing forth a different flavor of the teaching to match the mind of the seeker.

Here is the story:

In India, washermen are called *dobhis.* One day, as usual, a dobhi piled all his washing on the backs of his donkeys and herded them down to the river to begin work.

On his way there, he saw a hunter kill a lioness. The hunter skinned the lioness and then left. The dobhi discovered that the lioness had been pregnant. He saved the baby lion cub and raised it himself.

When the cub was big enough, he allowed it to run

---

* A version of this story was originally published in *Wake Up and Roar: Satsang with H. W. L. Poonja* (Eli Jaxon-Bear, ed.), Novato, Calif.: Gangaji Foundation, 1992.

about and play with his donkeys. Eventually, he started loading clothes for washing onto the young lion's back for the trip down to the river with the donkeys. So the lion grew up carrying washing on its back and being treated like one of the donkeys.

One day, a hungry lion came out of the jungle and saw the herd of donkeys grazing by the river. Donkeys are good food for lions. But among the donkeys there was a young lion, eating grass! The lion couldn't believe his eyes.

The hunting lion jumped out to confront the young lion and ask him what his problem was. In great fear, the young lion and all the donkeys ran off to hide in the bushes.

Finally, the big lion caught the little lion, who cried out in anguish, "Oh, please, Mr. Lion, don't eat me! Let me go back to my brothers, the donkeys."

The big lion said, "What are you saying? You are a lion!"

"Oh no, sir, I am a donkey. Please let me go!"

At this, the big lion grabbed the little one by the neck and dragged him down to the river. "Look in the water. Can you see our faces?"

"Yes," answered the young lion. "They are the same."

"Now open your mouth and roar!"

And the young lion opened his mouth and roared.

As he told this story, my teacher radiated the spiritual power of silence. He was the old lion of Lucknow,

India, an eighty-year-old Punjabi with blazing eyes shining from the very depths of the vast emptiness beyond time and space.

At the end of the story he would look at each one of us and ask, "How much practice was needed to become a lion?"

no practice necessary

Realizing your true identity is quite simple. It's not about practicing. There is nothing to transform. You're not going to *become* a lion some day. You just have to be willing to give up your practice of being a donkey.

Waking up is simply seeing life the way it *is*. It is nothing that you can create. When you stop creating and manifesting for at least a moment, what is left is what is already here prior to creation.

Again and again we hear the teaching: freedom means freedom from false identification — freedom from identifying as a donkey.

caught in donkeyhood

What keeps immortal consciousness caught in the belief in donkeyhood?

Historically, giving up donkeyhood has been rare, because life is relatively comfortable among donkeys. It's the life that parents have been teaching their children for countless generations.

But it is a deep trance; it is sleepwalking; it is the

subconscious, neurotic attachment to life as an animal. The fear is that if you wake up from a life as a donkey, you won't survive. How will you eat? What will you do? These are the donkey thoughts that flood the mind with panic at the idea of leaving donkeyhood.

After all, a donkey has no idea what a lion does. It can't imagine not being in the herd with all of the other donkeys. This is the trap: ignorantly identifying yourself as an animal, without noticing that the animal drives are subconsciously running the show. Below your conscious daily thoughts, a subconscious story rationalizes your motives and actions, showing why you're right to continue to do the donkey things that you do.

Finally, you come to a point where you've had enough — a point where you realize that what you thought you wanted never brings you true happiness. You can have more money, more power, more children, more status, more sexual partners, and more fame, but none of these make any difference if you continue to experience them as a donkey.

As long as you identify yourself as a donkey, you won't be happy. Since you are consciousness already, in the depths of your being you actually know that you're not a donkey. But because you are still subconsciously identified as a donkey, you continue to act like one, and this drives you mad.

Meditation practice does not necessarily lead to freedom; more often it leads to meditating donkeys.

Spiritual ripeness, the flowering of the full development of an individual, occurs when you see the horror of living life as a donkey, and recognize that you have been unable to end the identification.

whatever it takes

To realize who you are, the only thing required is willingness. You have to say to yourself, "Whatever it takes, I am ready. I am so fed up with being a donkey, I have to know who I really am!"

When your level of willingness reaches 100 percent, you realize the truth. If your willingness is partial, you get only a partial taste of truth. You have a few spiritual experiences, but the spiritual experiences only leave you hungry for more. Eventually, with maturity, you realize that all spiritual experiences come and go. If you try to grasp at truth, if you try to hold on to it, you will be disappointed, because spiritual experiences never last. You are left with the burden of a spiritual concept that gets used in defense of your story about why your life is the way it is. The experience of realization then becomes a burden, further veiling your true Self.

You can't make awakening happen. The donkey-identified ego can only make things happen that are in the realm of donkeyhood. Remember, it isn't the donkey who wakes up and realizes it is a lion. It is the lion who wakes up and realizes it has never been a donkey — it has always been a lion.

Let me ask you again: Are you willing to give up your neurotic addiction? The endless preoccupation with "me" and "my story"? The narcissistic/neurotic addiction to "What about me?" If so, you are ripe and ready.

beyond donkeyhood

The only thing required is for you to be willing to turn your back on slavery. This involves turning your back on everything you know.

Everything you know belongs to the realm of donkeyhood. Who you are is beyond knowing. To face the unknown, you are called upon to let go of your attachment to the known. You are called upon to see all the roles in your life as a donkey — the roles of child, father, mother, partner, employer, employee, male, or female — as mortal attachments, whereby immortal consciousness limits itself.

I am here to let you know that you're not limited. The possibility of freedom is open to you. Our faces are the same. Same face, same roar!

In the discovery of true Self, no magic rituals and no formal initiations are needed. Initiation into true Self happens quite naturally. When you drop your identity as a donkey, deeper levels of Self are revealed in silence. Once you have said, "Okay. It is time! Now is the time to find out the truth!" then all your attachments show up. These are your tests. These attachments are the tests of your willingness.

Whatever your tests may be, like the Buddha's they come tailor-made for you, because they are arising from your own mind. They threaten what you're most afraid of losing. When you lose what you're most afraid of losing, you discover that which cannot be lost. The only thing you can really lose is your false identification. True love is never lost.

being completely honest about what you really want

The first step in moving beyond donkeyhood is to be completely honest with yourself about what you really want. This is essential. Nothing is possible until you know what it is you really want. All unexamined, conditioned desires belong to your life as a donkey — desires for more food, more money, better sex, better children, better parents, better work — whatever they may be. All these desires and attachments happen in the kingdom of the donkey. Eventually you come to admit that no matter how many of your desires are met, ultimately, none of them leads to true fulfillment and freedom.

Once you understand this at the deepest level, you're willing to ask, "What do I really want?" This is the beginning. When you discover that what you truly want is bigger and more important than your personal life, you surrender to that which you want.

This surrender takes you. It is the beginning of a love affair with this unknown something, this something that is deeper than mind, deeper than thoughts, deeper than emotions, deeper than the body.

grace and fear

Grace appears in your story to call you into greater depths. With this surrender to grace, great fear often arises. This is the first test.

To attempt to escape back into the shallows of the mind means to run back to your donkey life. Either you run from fear by following a thought, or you fall into something unknown. If you're willing to fall into something unknown, then you can discover the ever-deeper truth of your Self.

silence

Freedom is discovered in silence. As the mind becomes more and more quiet, it gives up its attachments. As you discover peace in the depth of quiet, the fear that has been limiting the mind's exploration naturally loses its hold. The mind lets go of its hold on the past and the future. When you simply stop, in this moment, there is no past and no future. When there is no past and no future, there is silence. Exploring the depth of this silence leads to deeper realization beyond the borders of the known.

When your mind is quiet, love shines forth. Intelligent love is your nature. As soon as the subconscious attachment to donkeyhood disappears, love radiates. Since you aren't really a donkey, you don't have to work at being a better donkey. You don't have to learn to love and accept donkeyhood. This is the end of working on self-esteem and the beginning of true love of Self.

recognizing your lionhood

Remember, there are no donkeys, only lions pretending to be donkeys. A lion is always a lion, even if it is dreaming it is a donkey. The master's task is to tell the dreaming lion, "Look! We have the same face. Roar!" A true teacher is simply your own Self appearing in a different form.

The lion is a metaphor for the end of all thinking and the possibility of fully realizing your Self. Forget lions, donkeys, and humans. Let the whole universe disappear. When everything that has appeared disappears, you realize your Self as that which does not change. Then, when you incarnate in the apparent form of a lion, you quite naturally act like a lion. You don't need to believe yourself to be a lion. You don't have to remember who you are. One always is. You simply are.

Brothers and sisters, today is liberation day! Perhaps you have been like a slave who doesn't want to leave the slave district because it is so comfortable there. Perhaps you have been like the donkey, enjoying the walk to the river with the washing on your back, not noticing that you are a lion trapped in the sleepwalking trance of donkeyhood, claiming to prefer it because the trance is familiar.

The choice is yours. Nobody else can choose freedom on your behalf. Now is the time. You are a lion. In the words of Papaji: Wake up and roar!

epilogue

It has been fourteen years since the fateful day when I was led to my teacher's door. In that moment, all searching ceased. My mind stopped. All my prayers were answered. My life was fulfilled. I could die knowing that my mission was accomplished. I had made it home. I wanted for nothing, desired nothing. I told him all I wanted was to sleep outside his bedroom door and serve him.

Papaji made it clear that he had other plans for me. He said I would not believe what was in store. One evening we were out walking, holding hands as men do in India. His hand was eighty years old. It was large and had once been hardened by work. He had an *OM* tattooed between his thumb and index finger. He had driven jeeps and ridden motorcycles while working as a boss at a mine in the jungle before retiring at sixty-five.

His hands were softer now, the calluses smoothed over with age, and his touch brought tears of bliss to my eyes.

I said something to him about my awe at witnessing people arrive at his home and wake up in a matter of days. He said it is certainly amazing to see grace working, when a flame that is burning brightly lights another. What a mystery and joy.

"But," he added, "the candle that lights other candles that then light other candles — that is something else again!" With these words, he conveyed to me his mission and his holy work. He was lighting every candle in sight in the hope that the light would be passed on to all.

Papaji showed me how best to serve him. To serve him well is to pass on his precious gift to you, the reader. If you fully receive this gift and give your life to the burning love that you are, you may eventually realize that there is no giver separate from receiver — and in reality no act of giving. The "I" who writes these words in this moment is the same "I" who now reads them.

If you catch fire, then you become the candle that lights other candles. In this way, one by one, our world will come to the next stage of evolution and a return to sanity and peace.

All enlightened beings of all time and ages, of all lineages and traditions, are here in full support of you. Take good advantage of this precious moment. Who knows if it will come again? Now is your time. You are the one who has full responsibility for yourself, and now you have the knowledge and the choice. The rest is up to you.

We can all see the destruction of our world by the forces of ignorance, violence, and fear. You have the choice for the war to end where you are. Be yourself as love, and all peace-loving beings in the universe will rejoice in your awakening.

May there be peace and love among all beings.

All blessings are on you.

about the author

Eli Jaxon-Bear was born Elliot Jay Zeldow in Brooklyn, New York, in 1947. His eighteen-year spiritual path started in 1971, when he was a federal fugitive during the Vietnam War. In 1978, Kalu Rinpoche appointed him the president of his dharma center in Marin County. In 1982, he was presented with a Zen Teaching Fan at ChoShoJi Zen Temple in Japan. After studying many traditions and practices, his path and his search ended when he traveled to India in 1990, where he met his final teacher, Sri H. W. L. Poonja.

Confirming Eli's realization, his teacher sent him back into the world to share his unique psychological insights into the nature of egoic suffering in support of self-realization. He currently meets people and teaches through the Leela Foundation, an organization he established to further universal self-realization. He lives with his wife, Gangaji, in northern Caifornia. Eli is the author of *The Enneagram of Liberation: From Fixation to Freedom,* and editor of *Wake Up and Roar.*

The Leela Foundation is a nonprofit spiritual organization dedicated to world peace and freedom through universal self-realization, which sponsors retreats and professional trainings based on the sacred teachings of Self-inquiry and the Enneagram of Character Fixation.

The Leela Foundation
P.O. Box 1107
Bolinas, CA 94924
415-868-9800
website: www.leela.org

H J Kramer and New World Library are dedicated to
publishing books and audio and video products
that inspire and challenge us to improve
the quality of our lives and our world.

Our products are available
in bookstores everywhere.
For our catalog, please contact:

New World Library
14 Pamaron Way
Novato, California 94949

Phone: (415) 884-2100 or (800) 972-6657
Catalog requests: Ext. 50
Orders: Ext. 52
Fax: (415) 884-2199

Email: escort@newworldlibrary.com
Website: www.newworldlibrary.com